GREG L. HAWKINS AND CALLY PARKINSON

FOCUS

The Top Ten Things People Want and Need from You and Your Church

We Want to Hear from You

The purpose of REVEAL research is to provide church leaders with fact-based, action-able insights about spiritual growth. Your feedback is vital to our ongoing work. We encourage you to send us your questions and comments—about this resource or about anything else related to REVEAL. Direct your communications to cally@revealnow.com. Thank you!

PREVIEW

Church leaders often assume that what their people want is vastly different from what they need. Is this true? We start with three hypotheses to guide our research.

If you had to choose only one or two things for your church to do well, what would they be? What drives church satisfaction as well as spiritual growth? We identify the key to satisfying both wants *and* needs.

Senior pastors have a lot to do. Among all the demands they face, which tasks should take priority? Should they focus more on teaching or leading? We examine two key roles the senior pastor plays to determine which has the greater impact on spiritual growth.

When all is said and done, we need to know the bottom line. Here we look at the big-picture implications and practical applications of our research, summing it all up in two power-packed sentences.

Appendices

Greg L. Hawkins

THE LEADER'S DILEMMA: WANTS VERSUS NEEDS

It began in the Garden of Eden. God provided Adam and Eve with everything they needed—food, shelter, companionship, meaningful work. A gorgeous sunrise every morning and an even more spectacular sunset at the end of each day. But Adam and Eve wanted something else; they wanted to be like God. So they ate the forbidden fruit, and through that act, they were separated from God. Their lives were cursed, and they had to work hard to meet even their most basic needs.

Later, God provided his chosen people of Israel with judges— Ehud, Deborah, Gideon, Jeptha and others. Under their leadership, God's people experienced a season of peace and blessing. But they wanted something else. They wanted a king, "such as all the other nations have" (1 Samuel 8:5b). Reluctantly, God instructed the prophet Samuel to anoint Saul to give the people the king they wanted. But in time, Saul defied God's instructions, made several terrible decisions and died a tragic death. "And the LORD was grieved that he had made Saul king over Israel" (1 Samuel 15:35b).

God provided the disciples with the gift of his presence through daily fellowship with his son, Jesus. For three years the disciples witnessed countless miracles and heard Jesus bring the Scriptures to life like never before. But two of them, James and John, still wanted something else. "Let one of us sit at your right and the other at your left in your glory" (Mark 10:37). Jesus gave them a chance to reconsider, but they assured him that they knew what they wanted. However, what they needed was something else entirely. Jesus told them, "Whoever wants to become great among you must be your servant, and whoever wants to be first must be slave of all" (Mark 10:43–44). That sure doesn't sound like sitting on the left and right of a royal throne.

Time and time again, stories from the pages of Scripture reveal that what God's people wanted wasn't always what God wanted. Too often, getting what they wanted got God's people into a whole lot of trouble. Their wants blinded them to what they truly needed.

Too often, getting what they wanted got God's people into a whole lot of trouble.

✦ ✦ ✦

It began when you were born. What you wanted was precisely what you needed—food, a clean diaper, a nap, a hug from your mom, a smile from your dad. These are all good things. But somewhere around age two, your independence asserted itself and greedy little impulses took over. Everything you saw, you wanted. You reached, you grabbed. You used one word a lot—*mine*. As in "Mine! Mine! Mine!"

Then your parents introduced you to that most hated of two-letter words: *No*. You couldn't stand that word. In fact, you hated that word. And you didn't hesitate to let anyone within earshot know how unhappy you were whenever you heard it.

We like getting what we want. It is hardwired into our sinful little souls.

✦ ✦ ✦

It begins when they call you "pastor." Or elder, deacon, ministry leader—whatever name denotes your leadership role in the church.

Right away, people in the congregation start telling you what they want—more ministries, different music, deeper teaching, additional staff, a home visit. It isn't long before the realization hits that, given finite time and the church's limited resources—especially during tough economic times—you can't give everyone everything they want.

You wonder if what people want is really what they need.

In the back of your mind you also wonder if what people want is really what they need. You can recall a few times when God's people confused their wants with their needs, and you don't want to make the same mistake. And in the front of your mind is your daughter's request this morning for a cell phone, because "Everyone in fifth grade has one. I *need* one!" It makes you wonder if what your people want from you and the church might just be the spiritual equivalent of your fifth grader's cell phone.

How do you make sense of it all?

SORTING OUT WANTS AND NEEDS

Marketplace leaders don't have this problem. Most businesses focus intently on giving people what they want, and the best companies excel at it. "The customer is always right" is their mantra—just give people what they want and they'll reward you with their business.

But we aren't marketplace leaders, we're church leaders, and we know that this is not the way to lead a church. Our mission is to make more disciples of Jesus, not to give people what they want. Right?

So the first problem is sorting out wants from needs. Initially, that does not sound so hard, but after we've culled through all the requests and discarded the ones we should not do, we're still left with a rather long list of very real needs.

Now we need to prioritize all the things that are left on the list. We need a framework or a lens to guide those decisions. We ask ourselves, "What helped me find Christ and grow closer to him? What did I learn in seminary? What will have the biggest impact on spiritual growth? How do other church leaders do this?"

After wrestling through those questions, we're a littler clearer on what should come first and what we need to say no to, but it's not that simple. We still have to use great discernment as we navigate the organizational and relational dynamics of our decisions. If we say yes to Frank, who leads the men's ministry, how can we say no to Lori, who runs the compassion ministry? Saying no to a ministry volunteer, who sacrifices time and money, is a lot harder than saying no to your fifth grader.

Sorting out wants and needs is messy.

Sorting out wants and needs is messy. Over time, it can wear leaders down to the point that they're tempted to just give in and say yes to almost everything, whether or not that's really the right thing to do. Could there be a better way?

REVEAL

Over the past five years we have conducted research with thousands of congregants who attend churches all across America. We set out to learn what people really need in order to grow closer to Christ and become his disciples. Some of our initial findings were published in the books *Reveal* and *Follow Me*.

Recently, we set out to research what people really want from their church. We wanted to understand what motivated folks to show up in our churches every week. What did they want from their church experience? If we knew what they wanted from the church, then we could compare that to what we were learning about what they needed in order to grow spiritually. We believed this could help us understand whether or not there was an "expectation gap" between wants and needs. An expectation gap is the distance we as leaders must close in order to help our people get what is really best for them.

If the research revealed a small expectation gap between wants and needs, that would be good news for leaders in the church; if it revealed a large gap, that would not be such good news. For example, if I knew that macaroni and cheese was exactly what my kids needed to grow in a healthy manner and that it was also exactly what they wanted at every meal, then the nutrition part of my job as a parent would be a bit easier. But the gap between what my kids need and want is a lot bigger than that, and being a good parent means I can't just give them what they want. Instead, I need to be very intentional about closing the gap by feeding them things that are healthy but also taste good.

When we set out to research what people want from the church, our hypothesis was that the expectation gap between wants and needs would likely be large and we would then need to figure out how to manage the resulting tension. If people want one set of things and the church is giving them another, that's a recipe for disappointment— for us as leaders and certainly for the congregation.

We believe these discoveries will help you prioritize your time and limited resources.

To make things even more interesting, we also wanted to zero in on what people really wanted from their pastor. What did they want from the person at the top? How was that different from what they wanted from their church? And how did it match up with what they needed from the pastor in order to grow spiritually?

We were fascinated by what we discovered. We believe these discoveries will help you to prioritize how you spend your time and how you allocate the limited resources of your church. Our prayer is that what you read on the pages that follow will help you to focus in on how you can best serve the people in your church and help them grow closer to Christ.

After all, isn't that what you really want?

CALLY PARKINSON

FOCUS

1

THREE THINGS WE WANTED TO KNOW

hypotheses

CHURCH LEADERS often assume that what their people want is vastly different from what they need. Is this true? We start with three hypotheses to guide our research.

1

THREE THINGS
WE WANTED TO KNOW

What do people want? That's the question that drove the research for this book. When it comes to spiritual growth, we wanted to know what people *want* from the church and the senior pastor. We also wanted to identify what people *need* from the church and the senior pastor in order to grow spiritually. We were intrigued by the prevalent view among some church leaders that wants and needs are not necessarily compatible.

Our interest was sparked by feedback from senior pastors who expressed concerns about some of our initial research.[1] There were misgivings that efforts to measure satisfaction with the church and senior pastor were somehow inappropriate in the context of assessing congregational spiritual health. We felt that behind these misgivings were some missing facts about whether or not the factors that influence satisfaction with the church and the senior pastor are the same factors that inspire spiritual growth.

To address this concern, we structured a research inquiry designed to identify and compare what people want and need from the church and the senior pastor. On the pages that follow, you'll hear the collective responses of 80,000 people from 376 churches who took the REVEAL Spiritual Life Survey between October 2008 and March 2009. You'll read what we discovered about what they want and what they need from the church and the senior pastor in order to grow spiritually—and we think some of our discoveries may surprise you.

We wanted to compare what people want and need from the church and the senior pastor.

[1] Our initial research was published in Greg L. Hawkins and Cally Parkinson, *Reveal: Where Are You?* (Barrington, Ill.: Willow Creek Resources, 2007).

THREE HYPOTHESES

The purpose of a good hypothesis is to help guide the research.

All research starts with a set of hypotheses. A hypothesis is a theory, an assumption about what might be true. The purpose of a hypothesis is to guide the structure and the content of the research.

To develop our hypotheses about what people want and need from the church and the senior pastor, we drew on input from three sources: feedback from pastors about our first two books (*Reveal* and *Follow Me*); feedback from churches who have taken the REVEAL Spiritual Life Survey; and insights from more than 850 churches we surveyed over the past four years. Based on this input, we developed three hypotheses to guide our latest research:

1. *What people need from the church is spiritual guidance, but what they want is something different.*

2. *What people need from the senior pastor is spiritual challenge, but what they want is great preaching.*

3. *What people need from the church and the senior pastor is spiritual guidance and challenge, but what they want is a great weekend service.*

Our goal was to examine the responses from 80,000 congregants about what they need and want from their church and senior pastor so we could determine whether the data corroborated or refuted these hypotheses. Let's take a closer look at each one.

Hypothesis | 1

What people need from the church is spiritual guidance, but what they want is something different.

All of our research confirms that people need guidance to help them grow spiritually. When we speak of spiritual guidance, we mean that people need help building a foundation of core beliefs; they need help understanding how to read and interpret the Bible; they need help figuring out a pathway to guide their spiritual journey. For most people, the church is the primary source of that guidance, and it is especially important for people in the early stages of spiritual growth.

People need guidance to help them grow spiritually.

From previous research we know that people come to church for many reasons. Spiritual guidance may undoubtedly be one of those reasons, but is it the primary factor influencing people's satisfaction with the church? Any number of other factors—for example, Christian friends or crisis support—may be equally or more important.

In other words, we believe spiritual guidance is what people need in order to grow, but we're unsure about what they want. Our hypothesis reflects our suspicion that spiritual guidance would not be at the top of the list of what people want from the church.

Hypothesis 2

What people need from the senior pastor is spiritual challenge, but what they want is great preaching.

Our research has consistently confirmed that spiritual challenge is a key driver of spiritual growth. However, many pastors believe that even if people need spiritual challenge, what they really want from the senior pastor is great preaching. And based on feedback from these pastors, it's not at all clear that they think people associate "spiritual challenge" with great preaching.

It's not clear people associate "spiritual challenge" with great preaching.

Other factors might have a significant influence on people's satisfaction with the senior pastor. For example, we know many people are drawn to church when they experience loss or hardship. Might pastoral care rank high on the list of what people want and need from their senior pastor?

Drawing on feedback from pastors and our own speculations, we tested the hypothesis that what people need most from the senior pastor is spiritual challenge, but what they want is great preaching.

Hypothesis 3

What people need from the church is spiritual guidance and what they need from the senior pastor is spiritual challenge, but what they want is a great weekend service.

Based on what we heard from pastors, there appears to be nearly universal consensus that a church sinks or swims based on its weekend service. So what happens if the pastor's weekend message doesn't deliver spiritual guidance or challenge, which is theoretically what people need? Does that mean that people may get what they want—an enjoyable weekend service—but not what they need to grow spiritually?

connections

We wanted to explore the connection between what people want and need from both the church and the senior pastor in the weekend service. The prevailing view of the pastors we spoke to is that weekend services are central to satisfaction with both the church and the senior pastor, regardless of whether or not they deliver spiritual guidance or challenge. We crafted our third hypothesis to reflect this view.

continued on page 18

Cally Parkinson

What Does Satisfaction Have to Do with (Spiritual Growth?)

OUR GOAL IN THIS BOOK is to discover how churches and senior pastors influence spiritual growth. We approach this analysis in a number of ways, including an extensive assessment of what drives satisfaction with the senior pastor and the church. *What does satisfaction have to do with spiritual growth?*

To answer that question, we assessed the spiritual effectiveness of the churches in our database by looking at three things:

- How people feel about the church's role in their lives
- The spiritual attitudes people express; for example, their love of God and others
- Spiritual activities outside the church, such as personal spiritual practices, evangelism and serving those in need

We then identified the top 5 percent of churches that showed high levels of spiritual growth and effectiveness.

continued on next page

effectiveness

What Does Satisfaction Have to Do with (Spiritual Growth?) (cont.)

CHART 1-1 LISTS some of the characteristics we used to define spiritual effectiveness. The second and third columns on the chart detail the findings for the top 5 percent of churches compared with the rest of the database. The percentages indicate the highest possible response for each characteristic. In other words, when offered a choice of six possible responses, 37 percent of participants at the top 5 percent of churches chose

"very strongly agree"—the highest possible response—when asked whether or not their church challenges them to grow and take next steps.

The last column on the chart shows how much greater the results are for the top 5 percent of churches compared with the remaining churches. In essence, the percentages in the last column show how much the

Chart 1-1

Spiritual Growth Characteristics: Top 5 Percent of Churches
Compared to Remaining 95 Percent of Churches

How the Church Helps Me Grow Spiritually	Top 5% of Churches	Remaining 95% of Churches	Top 5% of Churches Have Results Greater Than Remaining 95% of Churches**
Challenges me to grow and take next steps*	37%	21%	+76%
Helps me understand the Bible in depth*	40%	25%	+60%
Helps me develop a personal relationship with Christ*	41%	26%	+58%
Spiritual Attitudes			
Love of God*	59%	40%	+48%
Love of others*	27%	17%	+59%
Willingness to risk everything for Christ*	44%	23%	+91%
Spiritual Practices and Behaviors			
Daily reflection on Scripture	32%	21%	+52%
Daily prayer	60%	48%	+25%
Serve those in need (once or twice a month)	56%	48%	+17%
Spiritual conversations with non-Christians (more than six in the past year)	36%	21%	+71%

*Percentage of people responding at the highest level (top selection out of six options) ** Percentages are calculated by dividing the response percentage of the top 5 percent of churches by the response percentage of the remaining churches and subtracting 1.

Chart 1-2

Satisfaction with the Church: Top 5 Percent of Churches
Compared to Remaining 95 Percent of Churches

a pattern emerges	Top 5% of Churches	Remaining 95% of Churches	Top 5% of Churches Have Results Greater Than Remaining 95% of Churches**
Satisfaction with the church's role in spiritual growth*	25%	15%	+69%

* Percentage of people responding at the highest level (top selection out of six options) ** Percentages are calculated by dividing the response percentage of the top 5 percent of churches by the response percentage of the remaining churches and subtracting 1.

remaining churches would have to increase their results in order to achieve the results of the top 5 percent of churches. For example, a 100 percent result in the last column would mean that the remaining churches would have to double their current results to achieve the results of the top 5 percent of churches. You can see that one of the numbers on the chart approaches 100 percent; the percentage who "very strongly agree" that they are willing to risk everything for Christ is 91 percent greater for the top 5 percent of churches when compared with the remaining churches. This means that the percentage response from the top 5 percent of churches—44 percent—is almost two times the response of the remaining churches—23 percent.

The top 5 percent

The top 5 percent of churches consistently report better results in all dimensions of spiritual growth. For seven out of the ten factors we measure, the top 5 percent of churches report responses that are at least 50 percent greater than the rest of the churches. Notably, evangelism through spiritual conversations is 71 percent greater in the top 5 percent of churches, and their people are 76 percent more likely to say their church challenges them to grow.

CHART 1-2 SHOWS that satisfaction with the church follows this same pattern. The top 5 percent of churches have much higher rates of satisfaction with the church's role in spiritual growth than the remaining 95 percent of churches.

This is not surprising. Clearly, churches in the top 5 percent demonstrate greater spiritual vitality than the other congregations. It is logical that people in these congregations would be happier with their church, and that is the case. The percentage of people responding that they are extremely satisfied with their church is 69 percent greater for the top 5 percent than the rest of the churches.

Does this mean that higher levels of church satisfaction drive spiritual growth? Not necessarily.

We are not implying that higher satisfaction with the church *causes* spiritual attitudes and behaviors to increase. However, we would say that higher satisfaction appears to be present in congregations that consistently report higher levels of spiritual maturity. Consequently, we conclude that gaining greater insight about what drives satisfaction may offer new and unique perspectives about the most effective ways for a senior pastor and the church to help people grow spiritually. ✦

WHAT YOU NEED TO KNOW

Before diving into the research findings in the chapters that follow, you will need to be familiar with two foundational concepts that shape all of our work: the spiritual continuum and the three movements of spiritual growth.

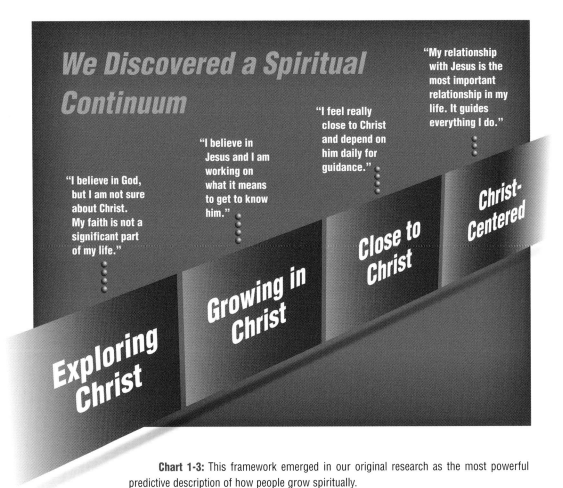

Chart 1-3: This framework emerged in our original research as the most powerful predictive description of how people grow spiritually.

The Spiritual Continuum

A primary objective of REVEAL is to understand the practical ways in which people grow spiritually. As a result of our research, we identified a way to probe people's attitudes, motivations and behaviors, and how to place them in one of four spiritual segments based on how important or central Christ is in their lives (chart 1-3).

Briefly, the four segments are as follows:

Exploring Christ
The people in this group have a basic belief in God, but they're unsure about Christ and his role in their lives.

Growing in Christ
The people in this group have a personal relationship with Christ. They've made a commitment to trust him with their salvation and for their eternity, but they are just beginning to learn what it means to be in a relationship with him.

Close to Christ
The people in this group depend on Christ daily for their lives. They see Christ as someone who assists them in life. On a daily basis, they turn to him for help and guidance for the issues they face.

Christ-Centered
The people in this group would identify their relationship with Christ as the most important relationship in their entire lives. They see their lives as fully surrendered to Jesus and his agenda, subordinating everything to his will and desires.[2]

We want to understand the practical ways in which people grow spiritually.

---

[2] For a more complete presentation about the spiritual continuum, see Hawkins and Parkinson, *Reveal.*

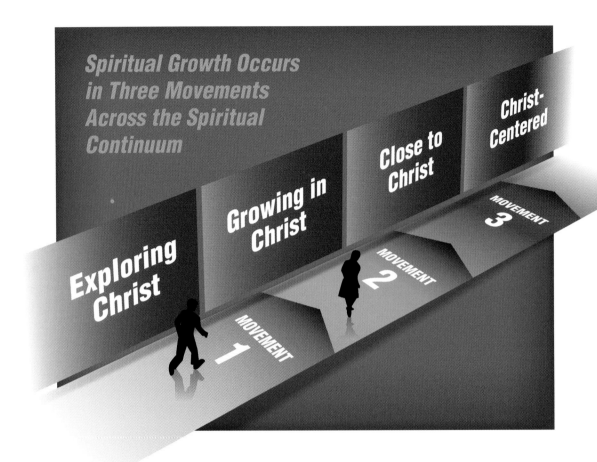

Chart 1-4: People progress across the spiritual continuum in three movements: Movement 1, early spiritual growth; Movement 2, intermediate spiritual growth; Movement 3, advanced spiritual growth.

Our ultimate goal is to understand how people actually grow to become more like Jesus.

The Three Movements of Spiritual Growth

Identifying the segments on the spiritual continuum gave pastors and church leaders a good framework to figure out where people are spiritually. But just knowing where they are is not enough. Our ultimate goal is to understand how people actually grow to become more like Jesus—in essence, how they move from one segment to the next on the spiritual continuum. We describe this as spiritual movement.

Here is a brief overview of how the three movements relate to the four segments on the spiritual continuum (chart 1-4).[3]

Movement 1:
The Earliest Stage of Spiritual Growth

In this movement, people gain their initial understanding of the Christian faith and accept that Jesus Christ offers the only path to salvation. They move from the Exploring Christ segment to the Growing in Christ segment. We know that establishing a strong foundation of Christian beliefs—like belief in salvation by grace and in the Trinity— is crucial for those in this early spiritual movement.

Establishing a strong foundation of Christian beliefs is crucial.

Movement 2:
The Intermediate Stage of Spiritual Growth

In this movement, people invest more time and energy into developing their own relationship with Christ. This is when they progress from Growing in Christ to a more intimate Close to Christ relationship. In this movement, personal spiritual practices—like daily prayer, reflection on Scripture and solitude—become a natural part of people's daily routines.

Movement 3:
The More Advanced Stage of Spiritual Growth

In this movement, a person's faith shifts from a daily awareness of Christ's presence (a Close to Christ relationship) to a redefinition of a person's identity based on their relationship with Christ (a Christ-Centered relationship). During this movement, we see significant increases in faith-based activities—like evangelism, serving those in need and engagement with spiritual friendships and mentors.

---

[3] For a more complete presentation about the three movements of spiritual growth, see Greg L. Hawkins and Cally Parkinson, *Follow Me: What's Next for You?* (Barrington, Ill.: Willow Creek Resources, 2008).

Think of the three movements as stages of a learning experience.

It might be helpful to think of the three movements as stages of a learning experience. For example, Movement 1, the earliest learning stage, would be like grade school; Movement 2, high school; and Movement 3, college. Just as a school curriculum creates a learning path that moves from basic to more complex coursework, the three spiritual movements also progress from basic to more complex spiritual experiences. Each movement depends on the spiritual groundwork laid in the prior movement, just like high school academics build on fundamentals learned in grade school.

The four segments of the spiritual continuum and the three movements of spiritual growth provide the foundation and primary framework for all REVEAL research findings, including those in the chapters that follow about what people want and need from the church and the senior pastor to help them grow spiritually.

This work builds on our previous research, which focused primarily on the most influential catalysts of spiritual growth; in other words, what people *need*. In this book, we focus on what people *want*—what drives satisfaction with the church and the senior pastor in promoting spiritual growth. We hope you will be both challenged and encouraged by what we discovered about the wants and needs that bring people to church.

CALLY PARKINSON

FOCUS

2

WHAT DO PEOPLE WANT—
AND NEED—FROM THE CHURCH?

church
satisfaction

IF YOU HAD TO CHOOSE only one or two things for your church to do well, what would they be? What drives church satisfaction as well as spiritual growth? We identify the key to satisfying both wants *and* needs.

2

WHAT DO PEOPLE WANT— AND NEED—FROM THE CHURCH?

Lists are useful tools. From simple to-do lists and daily calendars to more complex reference tools like telephone directories and restaurant menus, we make decisions and set priorities every day using lists. The goal of this chapter is to identify a list of what people want and need from the church to help them grow spiritually. Our hope is that this list will help you do three things that lists do very well—organize your thoughts, consider how to use your time and ministry resources most productively and help you focus on what's most important for your church.

The goal: to identify a list of what people want and need from the church.

To develop this list, we set out to research and compare two things: (1) the causes of church satisfaction and (2) the catalysts of spiritual growth. We wanted to know whether or not the biggest drivers of satisfaction with the church lined up directly, or not at all, with the biggest catalysts—or drivers—of spiritual growth. In other words, we wanted to see whether or not what people *want* from the church is, in fact, also what they *need* from the church to grow spiritually.

What do we mean by "drivers" of church satisfaction and spiritual growth? A driver is a strong force, something that creates significant energy and momentum. In golf, the driver is the club that creates the most force on a ball and sends it the longest distance. In our research, we were looking for the church's biggest drivers— those practices and characteristics that deliver the most force and have the greatest impact on both spiritual growth and satisfaction with the church.

Many believe there is a conflict between what people want and what they need to grow spiritually.

Many church leaders believe there is a conflict between what people want from the church and what they actually need from the church in order to grow spiritually. They often assume that congregants, like young children left to their own devices, would choose the spiritual equivalent of candy and computer games when what they really need is vegetables and outdoor exercise. They think that people prefer to be comforted and entertained at church, and would be happiest with a spiritual agenda that doesn't challenge them too much. We wanted to explore that assumption and find out if what people want (what drives church satisfaction) is indeed markedly different than what people need (what drives spiritual growth).

BUILDING THE LIST

To begin building our list of drivers, we drew on the foundation of over four years of extensive research with hundreds of congregations. We tested dozens of statements to gauge how well they describe what people need and want from the church to help them grow spiritually. Most recently, we tested sixteen statements and asked 80,000 congregants to rate each one in terms of its importance to them and their satisfaction with how well their church delivers that benefit.

A critical next step was to see if there were any natural clusters among the sixteen statements. Clusters are something like categories in the yellow pages of a phone book. Instead of listing hundreds of businesses alphabetically by name, the yellow pages cluster similar organizations together in large categories, like automobile dealers or hotels. This makes it much easier for people to sort through multiple options so they can focus on a specific set of items to meet their needs. Similarly, we wanted to create an accessible way to sort through lots of options so we could find and focus our attention specifically on the most significant ways the church drives satisfaction and spiritual growth.[1]

We don't want to miss the forest for the trees.

Why is it important to think about these statements in category clusters? Because we don't want to miss the forest for the trees as we try to determine the principal things the church must do to help people grow spiritually. Identifying categories enables us to keep the big picture in mind as we process the research findings.

At the same time, we don't want to lose sight of the proverbial trees— the sixteen statements themselves. They are very important, tangible expressions of what the church needs to do to inspire spiritual growth.

Five Big Categories

Our cluster analysis of the sixteen statements yielded significant results. It identified five big categories of things people expect their church to provide. In no particular order, they are:

- *Spiritual Guidance*

- *Belonging*

- *Accountability and Impact*

- *Ownership*

- *Serving*

[1] It's important to emphasize that we didn't predetermine these categories. In other words, we did not use our judgment or opinions to preassign statements to different groups. Instead, we used an analytical technique that links similar items together to see if any of the sixteen statements would sort themselves into natural categories. Drawing on all the data we collected, the analysis determined objectively which items were related to each other. If items are related to each other, it means they share similar statistical patterns. We tested the validity of these patterns in a second step in the analysis. For more information about this approach, see "Hierarchical Cluster Analysis" on page 106.

When we speak of what people *expect* from the church, we make very specific use of the term *expectation*. For the purposes of our research, we understand an expectation as something people think is likely to occur. It is not necessarily something they desire or want; nor is it necessarily something they require or need.

For example, when we visit a doctor for an annual physical, we expect to spend some time in the waiting room before a nurse calls us in for the appointment. We expect the doctor to do a thorough exam. We expect insurance to cover most of the bill. We expect these things to occur whether or not we *want* them to happen or *need* them in order to maintain our health.

something we think is likely to occur

This is our perspective in seeking to identify the expectations people have for the church. Once we understand what people expect from the church, we can assess which experiences they *want* most (what drives satisfaction), and which experiences they *need* most (what drives spiritual growth). ◆

In the pages ahead, we'll take a closer look at these five big categories—and the sixteen statements that align with each one—as we assess what people want and what they need from the church to help them grow spiritually. And we'll see if our findings support the first hypothesis we identified in chapter 1: *What people need from the church is spiritual guidance, but what they want is something different.*

WHAT PEOPLE EXPECT FROM THE CHURCH

To expect something is to think it likely.

These categories represent five expectations people have for the church's role in their spiritual growth (chart 2-1). We use the word *expectation* intentionally. To expect something is to think it likely. People naturally have expectations for what they think will most

Five Expectations People Have for the Church's Role in Spiritual Growth

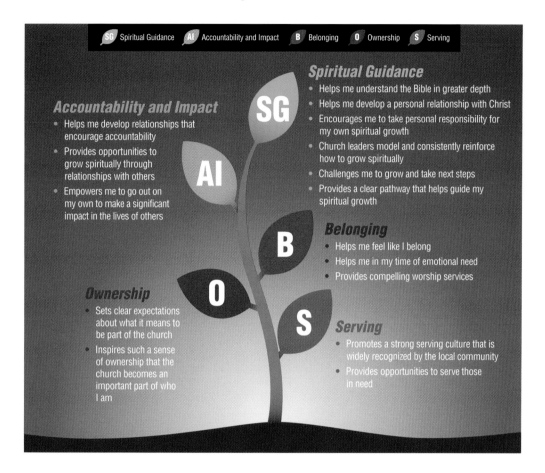

Chart 2-1: Our analysis demonstrated that these sixteen statements about what people expect from the church cluster together in five major categories.

likely occur in their church experience. These expectations are shaped by many things, including past experiences or experiences described to them by others. In essence, these categories reflect the range of expectations people have about what's most likely to occur when they go to church.

Spiritual Guidance

The six statements clustered in the spiritual guidance category express the expectation that the church will provide leadership for personal spiritual development. They include:

- Helps me understand the Bible in greater depth
- Helps me develop a personal relationship with Christ
- Encourages me to take personal responsibility for my own spiritual growth
- Church leaders model and consistently reinforce how to grow spiritually
- Challenges me to grow and take next steps
- Provides a clear pathway that helps guide my spiritual growth [2]

People expect the church to be their spiritual guide.

At the heart of this category is the expectation that the church will help congregants develop a personal relationship with Christ. People expect the church to be their spiritual guide, pointing them in the right direction and motivating them to move along that path.

Do people come to church hoping to know and become more like Christ? Our research suggests that they do. We know that a search for life purpose and a spontaneous interest in God are among the primary motivations for beginning to take faith seriously. This expectation for spiritual guidance speaks to how people hope the church will help them meet those needs.

Belonging

Belonging is about fitting in. Congregants want to experience community and worship in a place that helps them feel like they belong. The three statements connected with belonging include:

- Helps me feel like I belong
- Helps me in my time of emotional need
- Provides compelling worship services [3]

At first glance, it might seem odd to see "provides compelling worship services" in this category. We attribute this to the desire people have

---

[2] These statements are listed in random order. [3] These statements are listed in random order.

to belong to a church with a worship style that reflects their personal and cultural preferences.

All of us can identify with the need to feel like we belong. No one wants to feel awkward, lost or unknown in church. When we are at church, we want to feel like we are in a place where we are accepted and able to experience the ups and downs of life and spiritual growth in a supportive environment.

Belonging is about fitting in.

It might seem logical to associate a church's small group strategy with belonging. However, based on our research, we would suggest that belonging is less about feeling connected—which is typically a key objective of small groups—and more about affiliation. Affiliation means feeling like you fit in with a group of people and an environment. For example, lots of people affiliate with various sports teams. If you follow baseball in Chicago, you're either a White Sox fan or a Cubs fan. The experience of going to a game is all about being with a group of people who have a particular interest in common and enjoy participating in a shared event. Small groups appear to be more directly connected with the next category, accountability and impact.

Accountability and Impact

The accountability and impact category is about intentional spiritual relationships. Statements clustering in this category include:

- Helps me develop relationships that encourage accountability
- Provides opportunities to grow spiritually through relationships with others
- Empowers me to go out on my own to make a significant impact in the lives of others [4]

This is an others-oriented category that focuses primarily on the expectation that the church will help people develop relationships with others who will help keep them on track spiritually. Offering small groups is one church strategy to meet these expectations.

---

[4] These statements are listed in random order.

People expect a church to provide wise and trustworthy coaching about whether or not they are doing what they need to do to grow spiritually. People also expect a church to encourage them to have an impact on others, ideally in a variety of ways. This could include taking relational risks through evangelism or stepping out of normal routines to respond to the needs of others.

Ownership

Ownership is about allegiance and identity. Two statements describe the expectations people have for the church in this category:

- Sets clear expectations about what it means to be part of the church
- Inspires such a sense of ownership that the church becomes an important part of who I am[5]

At first glance, you might wonder about the difference between belonging and ownership. The difference is level of commitment. Belonging is about fitting in and feeling welcome; ownership is about having a personal stake in the church's direction and future.

"I am the church."

Ownership marks the shift from passive attendance at a weekend service to active engagement in the life and mission of the church. "I am the church" is the motto of those who very strongly agree with the value of ownership.

Serving

Serving expresses the expectation that the church will help those who are in need. Two statements cluster in this category:

- Promotes a strong serving culture that is widely recognized by the local community
- Provides opportunities to serve those in need[6]

People come to church with the expectation that serving those in need is central to the church's core values. That's a testimony to the

[5] These statements are listed in random order. [6] These statements are listed in random order.

role the church has played for centuries in the lives of those who find themselves in unfortunate circumstances.

The role the church plays is a unique one. In fact, many might say that, beyond weekend and holiday services, serving the underresourced is the most widely recognized activity and tangible expression of the church. For many it defines the church's character and consequently shapes the expectations of those who decide to participate in its activities.

The role the church plays is a unique one.

Having identified the five categories of things people expect from the church, I want to briefly revisit the sixteen statements that cluster around the categories. One way to understand the relationship between the sixteen statements and the five cluster categories is to think of the statements as sixteen specialized classes offered within five general academic subject areas. For example, in the subject area of mathematics, a student might choose to study geometry, algebra, calculus or statistics. All classes are important individually, and collectively they contribute to the student's expertise in mathematics. In the subject area of business, a student might choose to study accounting, marketing, management or operations. Again, all the classes are individually important, and collectively they contribute to a student's expertise in business.

This analogy helps us put these five categories and sixteen statements into proper perspective. The five categories function as the major subject areas that will keep us focused and on track as we process the research findings. The sixteen statements are like the specialized classes; they represent the tangible expressions of what the church has to deliver to create the five categories of spiritual experiences.

Now that we have identified the five expectations people have for the church, we'll take a closer look to see which ones emerge as the most powerful drivers of church satisfaction (what people want) and of spiritual growth (what people need).

WHAT DO PEOPLE WANT FROM THE CHURCH?

Ask a group of church leaders what people want from church and you'll likely hear a long and varied list of responses—not all of them positive. Church leaders routinely field e-mails, answer calls and engage in conversations with people who aren't shy about expressing what they want from the church. Topics can include the choice—and volume—of music, ministries the church should offer, topics the pastor should preach on and more. As important as such issues may be, they are not the focus of our analysis. Instead of focusing on topics that are about momentary sources of satisfaction or dissatisfaction, we wanted to focus on the larger issues identified in the previous section: spiritual guidance, belonging, accountability and impact, ownership and serving.

People aren't shy about expressing what they want from the church.

We wanted to understand which categories represent what people want most, and what truly drives satisfaction with the church's role in spiritual growth. Let me be clear. We're not focusing here on what people *expect* from the church or what they *need* from the church to grow spiritually. We wanted to know what they *want* most. Our focus here is on what makes people happy. And what we discovered surprised us in several ways.

Chart 2-2 illustrates the proportion of influence for each of the five categories on satisfaction with the church.[7] At 54 percent, spiritual guidance dominates the chart, which means it is by far the biggest driver of church satisfaction; it delivers the most force and has a much greater impact on church satisfaction than any other category. In simple terms, spiritual guidance has the biggest influence on how happy people are with their church.

We weren't surprised that spiritual guidance was important to satisfaction with the church, but we did not expect it to be so much more important than the other four categories. It also surprised us that serving didn't even appear, which means serving did not show up as

[7] For more information about the methodology used in this analysis, see "A Note about Pie Charts" on page 110.

Spiritual Guidance and Belonging Drive Satisfaction with the Church's Role in Spiritual Growth

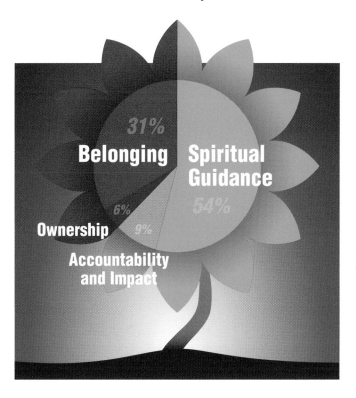

Chart 2-2: The spiritual guidance category accounts for the largest portion of the chart, which means it has much more influence than any other category on satisfaction with the church's role in spiritual growth. The belonging category is a strong secondary influence. These findings reflect responses from our total sample of 80,000 congregants from 376 churches.

having much impact at all on church satisfaction. After reflecting on the data, our analysis led us to five conclusions about what drives satisfaction with the church.

1. Spiritual guidance has by far the biggest impact on people's satisfaction with the church.

Spiritual guidance is the biggest driver of satisfaction with the church, representing more than half of the combined impact of all five categories. Its large influence probably reflects the truth of our earlier observation—that people come to church hoping to know and become more like Christ.

People want to know and become more like Christ.

Spiritual guidance is truly what people want from their church, which we hope encourages pastors who may sometimes feel frustrated by unrelenting complaints about things that seem to have little spiritual consequence. In fact, not only do people want spiritual guidance, its impact on satisfaction with the church is almost twice that of belonging, the next most influential category.

2. Belonging is also a powerful driver of satisfaction with the church.

Belonging is the second most influential category.

Belonging to a community of believers is a strong unifying force, which has a significant influence on church satisfaction. It accounts for approximately one-third of the circle of impact, which makes it the second most influential category after spiritual guidance. Its influence dwarfs the impact of the remaining categories.

3. The influence of accountability/impact and ownership on church satisfaction is limited.

Finding relationships that encourage accountability and feeling a sense of ownership for the vision and mission of the church are two categories that do not appear to have a significant influence on church satisfaction. This doesn't mean they aren't important elements of a person's church experience, but compared to spiritual guidance and belonging, they have much less impact.

4. Serving did not emerge as an influential category.

While no one would deny that serving those in need is an important church value, the fact that the church provides serving opportunities or a serving culture does not influence people's satisfaction with how the church helps them grow spiritually. How is this possible when serving the underresourced is so central to many churches?

The unfortunate but most logical explanation is that church satisfaction is driven by what's most important to personal spiritual growth, and serving others falls outside the scope of how people think about their spiritual growth experience. Satisfaction with the church appears to be derived from things that benefit individual spiritual development—like spiritual guidance and belonging—and serving doesn't seem to align naturally with those categories. So while people include serving in their expectations of what a church ought to do, an emphasis on service doesn't necessarily drive positive feelings about how the church contributes to their spiritual growth.

Does this suggest that people view church efforts to serve those in need with ambivalence or even reluctance? It may or may not. We can only conclude from the research that serving others is not on the radar screen for most people when they think about what makes them satisfied with how the church helps them grow spiritually.

5. The drivers of church satisfaction are the same for everyone—no matter where they are on the spiritual continuum.

No matter where a person is on the spiritual continuum—early in their spiritual journey or a mature Christ-follower—the biggest drivers of satisfaction with the church are the same.[8] This is a very important conclusion. It means that spiritual guidance is as important to someone who is Exploring Christ as it is to someone who is Christ-Centered. Similarly, a sense of belonging is as important to a veteran believer as it is to someone who is new to faith.

Spiritual guidance and belonging are what everyone wants from the church.

Because our results don't vary much at all by spiritual maturity, we can conclude that spiritual guidance is the primary driver of church satisfaction across the continuum and belonging is a strong secondary driver. Spiritual guidance and belonging are what everyone wants from the church.

[8] For more information about the spiritual continuum, see pages 18–19.

Having established what people *want* from the church, our next question is, What do people *need* from the church to grow spiritually? Which categories are most influential to spiritual movement from Exploring Christ to becoming Christ-Centered? And, more importantly, is what people want—spiritual guidance and belonging—also what they need?

WHAT DO PEOPLE NEED FROM THE CHURCH?

Wants are optional. Needs are essential.

The difference between a want and a need is significant. To want something is to desire it, like a craving for chocolate. To need something is to require it, like needing air to breathe. Wants are optional. Needs are essential. That's how we understand the difference between what people want from the church and what people need from the church to grow spiritually.

To determine what people need from the church to help them grow spiritually, we needed to identify which of the five categories were most directly correlated to three movements of spiritual growth.[9] These movements represent significant transitions from one segment to the next on the spiritual continuum:

Movement 1:
From Exploring Christ to Growing in Christ

Movement 2:
From Growing in Christ to Close to Christ

Movement 3:
From Close to Christ to Christ-Centered

---

[9] For more information about the three movements of spiritual growth, see pages 20–21.

Chart 2-3 demonstrates how the church influences spiritual growth in each movement. The first set of bars on the left indicates which categories are most influential for people who are at the beginning of their spiritual journey; the center set of bars shows what's most important for people in an intermediate stage of spiritual development; and the last set of bars on the right shows what's most influential for those who are more spiritually mature.

Spiritual Guidance and Accountability/Impact Drive
Spiritual Growth in All Three Movements

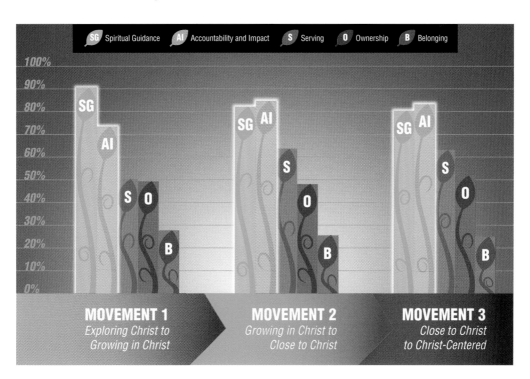

Chart 2-3: The influence of spiritual guidance and accountability/impact is illustrated by the tallest bars for all three spiritual movements. This means that spiritual guidance and accountability/impact demonstrate the greatest influence on spiritual growth for people at all stages of spiritual development.

The bars themselves indicate how important each of the five categories is to each spiritual growth movement. Spiritual guidance (the green bar) is the category that is the most influential catalyst for growth in Movement 1, the early movement of spiritual growth. This means spiritual guidance is the category of greatest impact. Belonging (the red bar), on the other hand, is the category that has the least influence on spiritual growth in Movement 1.

We reached the same conclusions for Movements 2 and 3. Both the intermediate and advanced movements of spiritual growth show the same pattern as the earlier movement—spiritual guidance and accountability/impact are most influential to growth; belonging is the least influential. This means that spiritual guidance and accountability/impact have the greatest impact on spiritual growth for all three movements, while belonging has the lowest level of impact.

We were unprepared for the influence of accountability and impact on helping people grow spiritually.

It didn't surprise us to find that spiritual guidance was so influential to all three movements. After all, we're trying to determine what the church does to drive spiritual growth, so providing spiritual guidance would seem like a no-brainer. But our findings uncovered other dynamics that did surprise us, and led us to the following three conclusions.

1. Spiritual guidance and accountability/impact are the church's most significant drivers of spiritual growth.

As noted, it was not a surprise that spiritual guidance had such a significant impact on spiritual growth. But we were unprepared for the influence of accountability and impact on helping people grow spiritually. It is the second most influential category in the earliest movement of spiritual growth—and it's also the most influential category in the intermediate and advanced spiritual movements. Again, what our analysis measures is the level of importance people attach to these five categories as they move across the spiritual continuum. This means that at every stage of spiritual growth, the accountability and impact category becomes increasingly important.

This strikes us as an insight that may be a great encouragement for church leaders. People appear to be aware that they have spiritual blind spots. They understand the need for relationships with trustworthy people who can offer thoughtful and constructive feedback on their spiritual challenges. This may suggest that many people possess an underlying humility and openness that makes them more receptive to spiritual guidance and coaching than church leaders might expect.

2. Serving and ownership are important contributors to spiritual growth.

Serving triggers spiritual growth.

While serving did not show up as a driver of church satisfaction, it is a very important contributor to spiritual growth for all three movements. This is consistent with previous findings about the importance of serving experiences as catalysts of spiritual growth.[10] Serving those in need naturally triggers spiritual growth when people act as Christ's hands and feet in settings that sometimes take them out of their comfort zones. Serving is an example of something people need from the church even if they don't want it, as noted previously in our findings about the lack of impact serving has on church satisfaction.

Ownership contributes to spiritual growth at approximately the same level as serving. This suggests that people acknowledge the importance of taking responsibility for the vision of the church as they grow spiritually. They understand that their role within the church should shift from observer, to participant, to full partner in advancing its work.

[10] For more information, see Hawkins and Parkinson, *Follow Me*, page 40.

3. Belonging is not a driver of spiritual growth.

Belonging was a very strong driver of satisfaction with the church, but it does not show up as a driver of spiritual growth. Why is that?

If you'll permit a gambling metaphor, we would say that belonging is like an "ante." An ante is the amount of money a card player puts into the pot before cards are dealt. An ante just gets you in the game—which is very important because you want to be in the game—but an ante doesn't help you win.

Belonging is what gets people in the game.

Belonging is often what gets people in the game when it comes to participation in a church, which is why it shows up as such a critical driver of church satisfaction. But belonging does not become increasingly important as people grow spiritually, which is why its impact on spiritual growth is minimal. Belonging is an example of something people want but don't necessarily need in order to grow spiritually. However, belonging is the ante that gets people in the door and keeps them coming back to the church, so it should still be a very high priority.

Now that we've analyzed what people want from the church and what they need from the church, we're ready to address the most important question of all:

> Is what people **want** from the church also what they **need** from the church to grow spiritually?

Based on our research, the answer is yes.

Chart 2-4 compares our findings about what people want from the church—the drivers of satisfaction with the church's role in spiritual growth—with our findings about what people need from the church in order to grow spiritually. Spiritual guidance dominates the circle of impact on church satisfaction (shown on the left), and it is one of two powerful drivers of spiritual growth (shown in the bar chart on the right).

Spiritual Guidance Is What People Want and What They Need from the Church

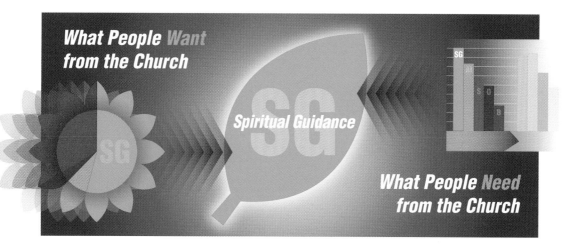

Chart 2-4: Two analyses—the first about the most influential drivers of church satisfaction and the second about the church's greatest influence on spiritual growth—independently reach the same conclusion. Spiritual guidance is what people want most from the church, and it is also the most effective way for the church to influence spiritual growth.

The impact of spiritual guidance on both church satisfaction and spiritual growth is compelling. While belonging is a strong secondary driver of church satisfaction and accountability/impact is a very influential secondary driver of spiritual growth, spiritual guidance is clearly the most dominant force driving both satisfaction and growth. This tells us that if a church must choose to do only one thing incredibly well, spiritual guidance is the runaway first choice.

As you'll recall from chapter 1, our first hypothesis was, *What people need from the church is spiritual guidance, but what they want is something different.* The first half of the hypothesis—that people need spiritual guidance to grow—appears to be correct. But the second half of the hypothesis—that they want something different from the church—appears to be incorrect. Spiritual guidance is by far the most influential driver of satisfaction with the church's role in spiritual growth. In sum, spiritual guidance is *both* what people want *and* what people need from the church.

Spiritual guidance is both what people want and what people need from the church.

FIVE THINGS EVERY CHURCH MUST DO—AND TWO MORE WE HIGHLY RECOMMEND

Spiritual guidance may be what people want and need from their church, but that's a pretty broad concept for a church leader to act on. It's like telling someone with a broken door that they need a toolkit in order to fix it. What the person really needs to know is precisely what tool they need—a hammer, a wrench or a screwdriver—and how to use it.

To make these findings more practical, let's circle back to the sixteen statements we talked about at the beginning of the chapter and focus specifically on the ones that are the equivalent of tools for the category of spiritual guidance.

The Spiritual Guidance List

Five statements produce and define spiritual guidance.

At the beginning of the chapter, I promised to give you a list that would help you organize your thoughts, use your time and resources productively and focus on what's most important for your church. Here it is (chart 2-5). In no particular order, it includes the five state-ments [11] that produce and define spiritual guidance:

- Helps me develop a personal relationship with Christ
- Challenges me to grow and take next steps
- Provides a clear pathway that helps guide my spiritual growth
- Church leaders model and consistently reinforce how to grow spiritually
- Helps me understand the Bible in greater depth [12]

[11] According to Chart 2-1 (page 29), spiritual guidance includes six statements, not five. We address the missing sixth statement on pages 48–49.

[12] These statements are listed in random order.

Five Characteristics Define Spiritual Guidance

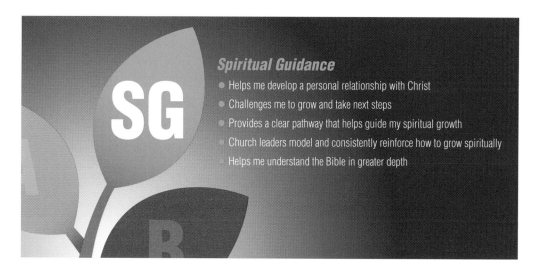

Spiritual Guidance
- Helps me develop a personal relationship with Christ
- Challenges me to grow and take next steps
- Provides a clear pathway that helps guide my spiritual growth
- Church leaders model and consistently reinforce how to grow spiritually
- Helps me understand the Bible in greater depth

Chart 2-5: These five statements represent the building blocks of the spiritual guidance category. They influence spiritual growth and also drive people's satisfaction with the church's role in spiritual growth.

These five statements reinforce each other and share many common characteristics. All of them speak to a need for the church to play a supporting role in assisting or encouraging spiritual growth in some way. The first statement expresses the desire for help in developing a personal relationship with Christ. While the statements that follow are not listed in any particular order, they read like a to-do list of how to help people make progress in this relationship.

The second statement expresses the desire to be challenged to take next steps. Taking next steps implies a pathway, which is described in the third statement. People want the church to show them the way, the route that will lead them to a Christ-Centered life. The fourth statement builds on that request by asking the church to demonstrate how to travel this journey. People want church leaders to show them—to model—what spiritual growth looks like. The fifth statement expresses the desire for help in accessing the biblical truths needed to guide and sustain the spiritual journey.

People want church leaders to model spiritual growth.

These statements are the tools you can use to provide people with the spiritual guidance they need. What do these tools look like in everyday ministry?

Here are just a few examples . . .

Provide a clear pathway to guide spiritual growth.

When you encourage people to develop personal practices that help them grow in their relationship with Christ—through daily prayer, solitude or journaling—you are delivering spiritual guidance.

When you challenge people to respond to biblical truth—through weekend messages and other communication channels—you are delivering spiritual guidance.

When you provide a clear pathway to guide spiritual growth—through membership or orientation classes—you are delivering spiritual guidance.

When you inspire leaders at every level to model and reinforce spiritual growth—through testimonies about spiritual struggles and dependence on Scripture for daily counsel—you are delivering spiritual guidance.

When you help people gain greater understanding about how to read and interpret the Bible—through teaching and classes and whatever other resources are available—you are delivering spiritual guidance.

These are the five things every church must do. When you focus the energy and resources of your church on making these five things happen, you give people what they want and need from the church, and you help them take next steps to draw closer to Christ.

Two More Statements to Pay Attention To

What about the rest of the sixteen statements? In particular, what about the statements we find in the belonging category, which is so important to church satisfaction; or the statements in the accountability and impact category, which is so important to spiritual growth? Are we saying that the activities represented by the five statements we just reviewed for spiritual guidance are enough—that a church can ignore the need to create an environment in which people feel like they belong, or where they find relationships that hold them spiritually accountable?

I wish we had a more definitive answer, but unfortunately the answer is both yes and no. Let me be clear about what we've discovered so far. We've concluded that if the church has to choose to do only one thing incredibly well, it should choose to do spiritual guidance with great excellence. The toolkit of spiritual guidance is made up of the five statements on chart 2-5 (page 45). However, if you want to maximize spiritual transformation in your church, we highly recommend adding two more statements to your spiritual growth toolkit: "Helps me feel like I belong" and "Encourages me to take responsibility for my own spiritual growth." Let's take a closer look at each statement.

Belonging is very high on the list of what people want.

Helps me feel like I belong.

Belonging is the second most powerful driver of satisfaction with the church's role in spiritual growth, which means it's very high on the list of what people want. However, when we looked at what people need in order to grow spiritually, belonging trailed all other categories.

We noted earlier that belonging is an ante; it gets you in the game. Evidence that belonging is a game-defining priority for the church lies in the fact that this statement—"helps me feel like I belong"—is as highly correlated with church satisfaction as the statements related to spiritual guidance. In other words, "helps me feel like I belong" is as critical to church satisfaction as any of the spiritual guidance statements. For this reason, we recommend including this statement on the list of top priorities for your church.

Perhaps this sounds like we're saying the church should give people what they want and not what they need. In this case, that's true. The bottom line is that there is a nugget of truth in the wisdom that a happy camper is much preferred over an unhappy camper. Happy campers are open to new thoughts, new ideas, new concepts—and they are your best recruiters of new campers. If the church helps people feel like they belong, they'll be far more open to spiritual guidance and they'll bring their friends and family along with them.

Belonging is about affiliation—about people feeling like they fit in. This means belonging is like the shoes people wear as they travel along the spiritual journey. If the shoes don't fit, the journey is slow and painful; but if they provide comfort and support, travelers will reach their destination much more quickly. Belonging may not drive spiritual growth, but a church that helps people feel like they belong will make that journey much more enjoyable.

Encourages me to take responsibility for my own spiritual growth.

This statement is included in the first cluster analysis of statements aligned with the spiritual guidance category (chart 2-1, page 29). Although it's a critical driver of spiritual growth, we found that this particular statement is not a driver of church satisfaction. In other words, this is something we know people need, but it is not something that they want. This suggests that telling people they need to take increasing responsibility for feeding themselves spiritually is a message that is very important, but may fall on deaf ears unless carefully communicated.

How do you inspire someone to do what they should do instead of what they want to do?

This statement presents to pastors the same dilemma parents face when they try to get their kids to eat apples and green beans instead of cookies and French fries. How do you inspire someone to do what they *should* do instead of what they want to do?

There's no easy answer to this; if there were, being a pastor (and a parent) would be a snap. The hard truth is that we must consistently develop creative strategies that motivate and equip people to take responsibility for their own growth. We need to make experimentation with new incentives and challenges a routine ministry discipline. And perhaps most importantly, we can't give up. We have to humble ourselves, roll up our sleeves and learn from each other.

We recommend including these two very important statements on the list of top priorities for your church. Doing so brings our original list of five priority statements to a total of seven (chart 2-6).

We must motivate and equip people to take responsibility for their own growth.

Five Things Every Church Must Do—and Two More We Highly Recommend

Chart 2-6: These seven statements are the essential characteristics of churches that provide people with what they want and need for spiritual growth.

These seven statements define what people want and need from the church to help them grow spiritually. People want and need the church to be their spiritual guide, pointing them in the right direction and motivating them to move along that path. Churches who deliver the activities, teaching, counsel and encouragement that bring all of these statements to life will create an irresistible spiritual momentum.

FROM HYPOTHESIS TO DECLARATION

People crave spiritual guidance.

We began this chapter with a theory, a hypothesis of what we thought might be true about the relationship between what people want and need from the church: *What people need from the church is spiritual guidance, but what they want is something different.*

Using that hypothesis, we discovered seven statements (chart 2-6, page 49), which only partially supported our hypothesis. As a more accurate reflection of our findings, we offer this declaration: *What people need and want from the church is spiritual guidance.*

This declaration acknowledges that people need all the things included in the spiritual guidance category in order to grow. It also acknowledges that spiritual guidance is the dominant driver of satisfaction with the church. People crave spiritual guidance.

Five imperatives plus two priorities

The seven statements on chart 2-6 represent the five imperatives of spiritual guidance plus two priorities we highly recommend for every church. This is the list promised at the beginning the chapter—a list we hope will serve as a framework for organizing your thoughts, for using your time and resources most productively and for focusing the ministry of your church on the things that are most important to the spiritual growth of your congregation.

CALLY PARKINSON

FOCUS

WHAT DO PEOPLE WANT—
AND NEED—FROM THE SENIOR PASTOR?

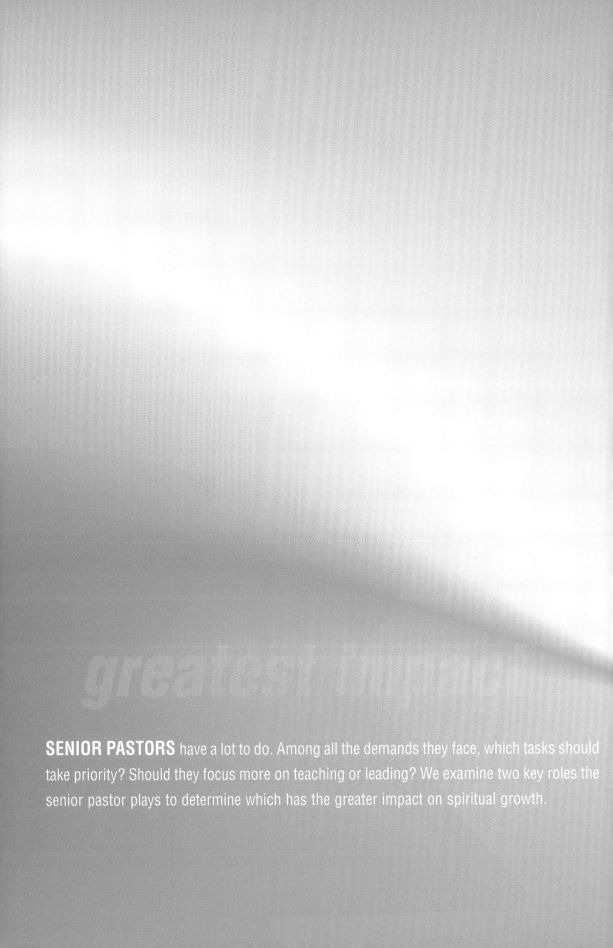

SENIOR PASTORS have a lot to do. Among all the demands they face, which tasks should take priority? Should they focus more on teaching or leading? We examine two key roles the senior pastor plays to determine which has the greater impact on spiritual growth.

3

WHAT DO PEOPLE WANT—AND NEED—FROM THE SENIOR PASTOR?

If there's anyone with limited time, energy and resources, it's a senior pastor. So the goal of this chapter is to deliver two tools to help a senior pastor manage time and resources most effectively. First, we'll deliver a list of the senior pastor's top priorities to help people grow spiritually. This list will feature the top things people need from a senior pastor for spiritual growth and the top things that drive satisfaction with the senior pastor. Are they the same? We'll see.

Then we'll determine which senior pastor role—the role of teacher or leader—is more influential in helping people grow spiritually. When we are done, a senior pastor should have a very good handle on which role delivers the most impact on spiritual growth, as well as specific direction on what people need most from a senior pastor to grow spiritually.

To get at the heart of the senior pastor's responsibilities, we tested seventeen statements, asking 80,000 people in 376 churches to rate each statement in terms of its importance to the senior pastor's role and also their satisfaction with how well their senior pastor fulfilled each responsibility.

Drawing on the same analytical technique described in chapter 2 (pages 26–27), we wanted to see if there were any natural cluster categories among the seventeen statements. Clustering the statements into categories is important because it enables us to sort through multiple options so we can focus our attention on the most

The goal: to help a senior pastor manage time and resources most effectively.

significant ways the senior pastor drives both satisfaction and spiritual growth. What emerged were six big categories that describe what people view as the senior pastor's primary responsibilities. In no particular order, they are:

- *Serving Advocacy*

- *Spiritual Challenge*

- *Pastoral Care*

- *External Focus*

- *Preaching and Vision Casting*

- *Unity and Stability*

To get a clearer picture of what people want and need from the senior pastor, we'll begin by focusing on these six categories, then we'll circle back to the seventeen statements that align with each category. And we'll see what our findings have to say about our final two hypotheses:

- What people need from the senior pastor is spiritual challenge, but what they want is great preaching.
- What people need is spiritual guidance from the church and spiritual challenge from the senior pastor, but what they want is a great weekend service.

We'll explore and assess both hypotheses through the lens of our findings about the senior pastor. Our goal is to provide new insight and understanding about which senior pastor roles and responsibilities have the greatest impact on spiritual growth, and whether those roles and responsibilities are consistent with what people want (what drives senior pastor satisfaction).

WHAT DO PEOPLE EXPECT FROM THE SENIOR PASTOR?

When people walk into a church, they have expectations about nearly everything they will encounter there, including the senior pastor. These expectations are not necessarily what people want or need from a senior pastor; they are more like components of a senior pastor job description—a collection of things people think are most likely to be involved in the role of a senior pastor.

People have expectations about nearly everything they will encounter at church.

The six categories identified by our cluster analysis reflect what people expect the senior pastor to provide (chart 3-1).

Six Expectations People Have for the Senior Pastor

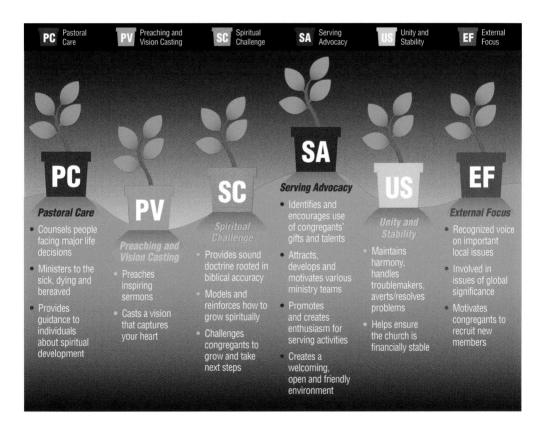

PC Pastoral Care   **PV** Preaching and Vision Casting   **SC** Spiritual Challenge   **SA** Serving Advocacy   **US** Unity and Stability   **EF** External Focus

PC Pastoral Care
- Counsels people facing major life decisions
- Ministers to the sick, dying and bereaved
- Provides guidance to individuals about spiritual development

PV Preaching and Vision Casting
- Preaches inspiring sermons
- Casts a vision that captures your heart

SC Spiritual Challenge
- Provides sound doctrine rooted in biblical accuracy
- Models and reinforces how to grow spiritually
- Challenges congregants to grow and take next steps

SA Serving Advocacy
- Identifies and encourages use of congregants' gifts and talents
- Attracts, develops and motivates various ministry teams
- Promotes and creates enthusiasm for serving activities
- Creates a welcoming, open and friendly environment

US Unity and Stability
- Maintains harmony, handles troublemakers, averts/resolves problems
- Helps ensure the church is financially stable

EF External Focus
- Recognized voice on important local issues
- Involved in issues of global significance
- Motivates congregants to recruit new members

Chart 3-1: Our analysis demonstrated that these seventeen statements about what people expect from their senior pastor cluster together in six major categories.

Serving Advocacy

Serving advocacy is the expectation that the senior pastor is the chief promoter and champion of serving opportunities. The four statements included in serving advocacy are:

- Identifies and encourages use of congregants' gifts and talents
- Attracts, develops and motivates various ministry teams
- Promotes and creates enthusiasm for serving activities
- Creates a welcoming, open and friendly environment [1]

Whether the need is for volunteers to serve in the children's ministry or to help out at the local food pantry, people expect the senior pastor to be a vocal and visible advocate on behalf of the church's ministries and ministry partners.

People expect the senior pastor to be a vocal and visible advocate.

At first glance, creating a welcoming environment might seem like an odd fit on a list related to serving advocacy. Although we don't have a definitive explanation, our speculation is that people may associate the most visible serving positions in the church—such as greeters and ushers—with the senior pastor's responsibility to establish a welcoming environment.

The senior pastor is seen as someone who intercedes on behalf of ministries that need volunteers and resources. This might include anything from asking people to contribute their time or money to encouraging people to discover and use their spiritual gifts in serving others.

Due to the senior pastor's unique position as the church's most visible spokesperson and spiritual shepherd, people naturally assume that advocating the Christlike value of serving others is one of the senior pastor's key roles.

[1] These statements are listed in random order.

Spiritual Challenge

Spiritual challenge tells us that people expect the senior pastor to be their spiritual leader. The three statements that define spiritual challenge capture the essence of this role:

- Provides sound doctrine rooted in biblical accuracy
- Models and reinforces how to grow spiritually
- Challenges congregants to grow and take next steps [2]

A central assumption is that the senior pastor will provide sound doctrine that is biblically accurate. This means the senior pastor is viewed as the church's theological spokesperson and expert.

People also expect the senior pastor to set an example: to model and reinforce through testimony and daily interactions what it looks like to intentionally pursue spiritual growth. As the theological expert and spiritual role model, the senior pastor is the one people expect to challenge them to take their next steps toward spiritual maturity.

Challenge is the key element of this expectation. Because of the senior pastor's perceived biblical expertise and life experience on a spiritual journey, people grant permission to the senior pastor to confront them, to test them and to persuade them to take whatever steps they need to take to grow into a disciple of Christ.

People expect the senior pastor to be the church's theological expert and spiritual role model.

Pastoral Care

The expectation for pastoral care means the senior pastor is seen as the spiritual shepherd of the human soul. Expectations about the role of pastoral caregiver are based on three statements related to the responsibilities of spiritual guidance and counseling:

- Counsels people facing major life decisions
- Ministers to the sick, dying and bereaved
- Provides guidance to individuals about spiritual development [3]

---

[2] These statements are listed in random order.   [3] These statements are listed in random order.

These statements focus primarily on the expectation that the senior pastor will provide support for those facing difficult decisions and circumstances. When people experience suffering—grief, dislocation, pain—they naturally turn to their senior pastor for comfort, counsel and guidance. Interestingly, the need for the senior pastor to provide guidance for spiritual development also aligns with this expectation for pastoral care, which may indicate that people appreciate the need for a strong faith to help them navigate the challenges of life.

People turn to their senior pastor for comfort, counsel and guidance.

External Focus

External focus is the expectation that the senior pastor is the spiritual ambassador for the church. The three statements that define external focus are:

- Recognized voice on important local issues
- Involved in issues of global significance
- Motivates congregants to recruit new members [4]

People expect the senior pastor to represent the church to other organizations and leaders. They also expect the senior pastor to be a cheerleader for community outreach, urging congregants to bring new members into the church. And people expect the senior pastor to encourage the church's engagement with local community concerns as well as issues of national and global significance.

These concerns might focus on humanitarian issues, such as the HIV/AIDS pandemic or local homelessness, or on political and social justice issues, such as race relations. We can all think of senior pastors who have taken strong public positions and had great influence on such issues. Public awareness of church leaders who are active in external concerns contributes to the expectation that it is appropriate for a senior pastor to focus attention on issues beyond the walls of the church.

[4] These statements are listed in random order.

Preaching and Vision Casting

The expectation for preaching and vision casting relates to the senior pastor's role as spiritual professor and spokesperson for the vision of the church. The two statements that define preaching and vision casting are:

- Preaches inspiring sermons
- Casts a vision that captures your heart [5]

This role likely demands more time and attention from the senior pastor than any other responsibility. As the primary teacher at weekend services, the senior pastor is the church's main source of spiritual education, enlightenment, inspiration and encouragement. The senior pastor is also the one responsible for painting a picture of the hopes and dreams of the church. This role includes casting a vision for the church's future that captures people's hearts and motivates ministry leaders and congregants to actively participate in achieving it.

The senior pastor is the church's main source of spiritual education and inspiration.

Unity and Stability

The category of unity and stability expresses the expectation that the senior pastor is the church's recognized leader. In other words, people expect the senior pastor to be more than a spokesperson for the church's direction and future. They also expect the senior pastor to provide leadership and make the decisions to ensure the church remains financially secure and free of conflict. The two statements that define this category are:

- Maintains harmony, handles troublemakers, averts/resolves problems
- Helps ensure the church is financially stable [6]

People see the senior pastor as a stabilizing force, both in terms of managing the church's finances with integrity and holding accountable those who have leadership positions within the church.

[5] These statements are listed in random order.   [6] These statements are listed in random order.

Congregants also expect the senior pastor to facilitate and maintain harmony among those in the church community.

Now that we've identified the six categories of things people expect from the senior pastor, let's briefly revisit the seventeen statements that cluster around each of the categories. As noted in chapter 2, the relationship between the six cluster categories and the seventeen statements is similar to the relationship between general academic subject areas and the specific classes offered within those subject areas. For example, in the subject area of science, a student might choose to study chemistry, biology or physics. The classes are individually important, and collectively they contribute to a student's expertise in the area of science.

Likewise, when it comes to the things people want from the senior pastor to help them grow spiritually, the six categories function as the major subject areas that will keep us focused and on track as we process the research findings. The seventeen statements are like the specialized classes; they represent the tangible expressions of what the senior pastor has to deliver to fulfill the responsibilities represented by the six categories.

In the next two sections, we'll take a closer look to see which categories emerge as the most powerful drivers of senior pastor satisfaction (what people want) and of spiritual growth (what people need).

WHAT DO PEOPLE WANT FROM THE SENIOR PASTOR?

Reading through the list of expectations people have for a senior pastor, it's hard to imagine anyone would want the job. People seem to expect a senior pastor to be everything from a brilliant communicator and savvy chief executive to a compassionate caregiver. However, we suspect that out of this whole package of impossibly high expectations, some roles will emerge as more important than others. Among all the things people expect a senior pastor to provide, which do they want most? In other words, which roles are most likely to make people happy with their senior pastor?

People seem to expect a senior pastor to be everything.

Preaching and Vision Casting Drive Satisfaction with the Senior Pastor

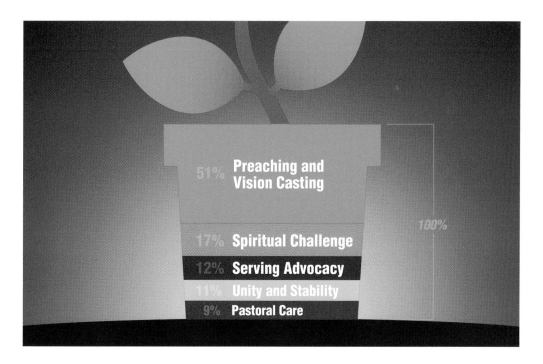

Chart 3-2: The preaching and vision casting category accounts for the largest portion of the chart, which means it has much more influence than any other category on satisfaction with the senior pastor. In fact, it has three times the influence of any other category. These findings reflect responses from our total sample of 80,000 congregants in 376 churches.

Chart 3-2 (page 61) illustrates how much influence each of the six categories has on satisfaction with the senior pastor.[7] Some of these findings didn't surprise us, but others were unexpected.

We were not surprised that the category of preaching and vision casting was the biggest driver of satisfaction with the senior pastor. However, we were surprised by its dominant influence—51 percent—when compared with the other five categories. In particular, we thought that pastoral care might have a more significant influence since so many people are drawn to the church for support during difficult life circumstances. We were also surprised that external focus had no impact whatsoever on satisfaction with the senior pastor. After reflecting on these findings, we arrived at five conclusions about what drives satisfaction with the senior pastor.

1. Preaching and vision casting have the biggest impact on satisfaction with the senior pastor.

External focus had no impact on satisfaction with the senior pastor.

The category of preaching and vision casting represents the biggest driver of satisfaction with the senior pastor, accounting for more than half of the influence of all six categories. In other words, this is what people want most from their senior pastor. It is not surprising that this category had the greatest influence on satisfaction, but considering all the other things people expect from the senior pastor, the extent of its impact is remarkable. Its influence is three times greater than the next largest category.

2. Spiritual challenge is a secondary influence on satisfaction with the senior pastor.

Spiritual challenge captures the desire people have for the senior pastor to be the church's chief theologian and a spiritual role model. While it is without a doubt very important, spiritual challenge emerged as secondary to the enormous influence of preaching and

---

[7] For more information about the methodology used in this analysis, see "A Note about the Pie Charts" on page 110.

vision casting. And the difference between the two is sizeable—17 percent for spiritual challenge and 51 percent for preaching and vision casting. The category of preaching and vision casting has three times the impact of spiritual challenge on satisfaction with the senior pastor.

3. Pastoral care, unity/stability and serving advocacy combined have less impact on satisfaction with the senior pastor than preaching and vision casting alone.

These three areas of senior pastor responsibility are very important, but their impact on satisfaction with the senior pastor pales in comparison to the impact of preaching and vision casting. In combination they account for 32 percent, about one-third of the total influence of all six categories, whereas the preaching and vision-casting category accounts for over one half. Interestingly, each one of these three categories has a similar level of influence; in other words, none is much more influential than the other two.

4. External focus does not influence satisfaction with the senior pastor.

The senior pastor's role as an influential voice in the local community and as an advocate for issues of national and global significance may be something people expect, but they don't seem to give the senior pastor much credit for it. Based on our analysis, external focus has no positive influence on satisfaction with the senior pastor.

Does this suggest that congregants have a somewhat self-centered or parochial point of view? Do they resent the time and energy their senior pastor spends on issues that don't directly impact the church? While this could be one possible explanation, our research can only conclude that the impact of external focus on senior pastor satisfaction is at best neutral compared with the other categories, all of which have positive impacts.

5. The drivers of senior pastor satisfaction are the same for everyone—no matter where they are on the spiritual continuum.

Our analysis shows that what people want from the senior pastor does not differ based on their spiritual maturity. This means that whether someone is in the early stages of Exploring Christ or is deeply Christ-Centered, the biggest driver of senior pastor satisfaction is preaching and vision casting.[8] So we can conclude that the category of preaching and vision casting is the primary driver of senior pastor satisfaction across the continuum, and that all other categories are distant runners-up in terms of impact.

What people want from the senior pastor does not differ based on their spiritual maturity.

Consider some of the challenging implications of this finding. We know from our research that every church includes people who are in all four segments on the spiritual continuum. And this finding tells us that everyone, whatever their stage of spiritual maturity, comes to church with high expectations for what they will hear from the senior pastor. That means that the senior pastor is responsible every week for preaching one message to a group of people who are at very different stages of spiritual growth. Preparing an effective spiritual message for such a diverse crowd is like preparing a math lesson for a group of students with education levels ranging from grammar school to college. It would be impossible to be equally effective for all of them. Yet that is the reality senior pastors face every time they get up to preach.

---

[8] For more information on the spiritual continuum, see pages 18–19.

Now that we've established that people definitely want great preaching and vision casting from their senior pastor, our next question is, What do people need from the senior pastor in order to grow spiritually? And is what they want also what they need?

WHAT DO PEOPLE NEED FROM THE SENIOR PASTOR?

As chief theologian and spiritual guide for the congregation, the senior pastor provides Christian instruction and modeling that influence hundreds, if not thousands, of people over a lifetime. That's a hefty responsibility all by itself—but there's more. The senior pastor is also the church's commander-in-chief, responsible for a wide range of short- and long-term decisions that chart the course of the church and impact people's lives in significant ways. In light of everything a senior pastor is responsible for, what are the most important things a congregation needs from the senior pastor to help them grow spiritually?

The senior pastor is the church's commander-in-chief.

To determine what people need most from the senior pastor, we identified which of the six categories were the most influential to the three movements of spiritual growth.[9] These movements represent significant transitions from one segment to the next on the spiritual continuum:

---

[9] For more information about the three movements of spiritual growth, see pages 20–21.

Movement 1:
From Exploring Christ to Growing in Christ

Movement 2:
From Growing in Christ to Close to Christ

Movement 3:
From Close to Christ to Christ-Centered

Spiritual Challenge Drives Spiritual Growth in All Three Movements

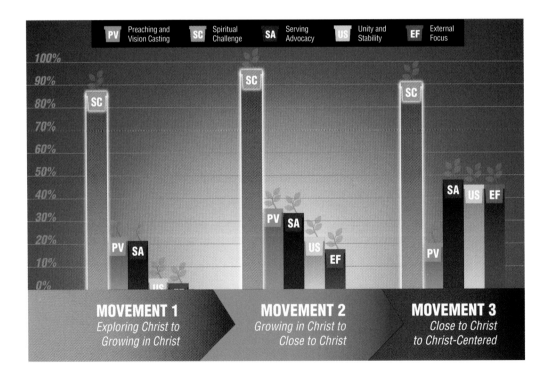

Chart 3-3: The influence of spiritual challenge is illustrated on this chart by the tallest bar for all three spiritual movements. This means that spiritual challenge demonstrates the greatest influence on spiritual growth for people in all stages of spiritual development.

Chart 3-3 illustrates how the senior pastor influences spiritual growth in each movement. The first set of bars on the left shows the categories that are most influential for people who are at the beginning of their spiritual journey; the center set of bars indicates what's most important for people in an intermediate stage of spiritual development; and the set of bars on the right represents what's most influential for those who are more spiritually mature.

Wow!

The findings are dramatic. Spiritual challenge (the orange bar) has by far the most powerful effect on spiritual growth for all three movements. No other category comes close to its level of impact—including preaching and vision casting, which dominated the analysis about what drives satisfaction with the senior pastor. This means that, while great preaching and vision casting is definitely what people want from the senior pastor, it is not—by itself—particularly influential to spiritual growth. On the other hand, spiritual challenge—delivered through teaching, counseling or leading the church—is clearly what people need from the senior pastor in order to grow.

We were not surprised that spiritual challenge showed up as the senior pastor responsibility most influential to spiritual growth. However, its level of dominance compared to the other categories did surprise us, particularly in the more mature stages of spiritual growth. It makes sense that spiritual challenge would be critical to those who are early in their spiritual journey; they would naturally look to the senior pastor to encourage their first steps of spiritual exploration. But the fact that spiritual challenge continues to be so dramatically important for all three spiritual movements implies that even those most firmly rooted and secure in their relationship with Christ depend on the senior pastor to challenge and encourage their spiritual progress.

Spiritual challenge has by far the most powerful effect on spiritual growth.

As we reflected more on these findings, we drew three conclusions about what people need most from their senior pastor to help them grow spiritually.

1. Spiritual challenge is the senior pastor's most significant driver of spiritual growth.

The influence of spiritual challenge is dramatic.

The level of impact and influence of spiritual challenge across all three movements is dramatic. Based on our previous research, we know that the most important next steps people need to take to grow spiritually differ significantly depending on their level of spiritual maturity. Yet the most important responsibility for the senior pastor is to challenge all of them, even though the next spiritual growth step for one person could be very different from the next step for someone else. For example, we know that establishing core beliefs is essential to Movement 1; personal spiritual practices are critical to Movement 2; and spiritual activities like evangelism and serving the underresourced spur growth for those in Movement 3.[10]

This is a very important, but somewhat unsettling, insight for a senior pastor. When people have such wide-ranging spiritual needs, challenging them with clear and effective next steps can be a complicated task.

[10] For more information about what catalyzes spiritual growth in all three movements, see Hawkins and Parkinson, *Follow Me.*

2. The most spiritually mature people need more from a senior pastor to help them grow than those at earlier stages of spiritual development.

While the role of spiritual challenge has the greatest influence on spiritual growth for all movements, we note that three other categories of senior pastor responsibilities also rise in importance. In fact, in the most advanced movement, three responsibilities—serving advocacy, unity and stability and external focus—show up as highly influential. One implication of this finding may be that these more mature Christians have a greater personal stake in the church. Consequently, the roles of providing unity and stability as well as serving advocacy are increasingly important to them. They need spiritual challenge, to be sure, but they also need to see more and different types of leadership from the senior pastor.

More mature Christians have a greater personal stake in the church.

They also see external focus as an increasingly important role for the senior pastor. This is true even though, based on the findings in the previous section, external focus is not something that they want; in other words, it doesn't influence their satisfaction with the senior pastor. This could explain why pastors may at times feel they are fighting an uphill battle to engage congregants in addressing concerns beyond the walls of the church.

3. Pastoral care does not contribute to spiritual growth.

The pastoral care category is missing on chart 3-3 because it does not influence spiritual growth. This means that pastoral care did not become increasingly important for any of the spiritual growth movements. This is not surprising because pastoral care is likely viewed as something people need at particular times—for example, during a life crisis—rather than something they need in increasing measure to spur on spiritual growth.

✦ ✦ ✦

We now have a dilemma.

Having reviewed all the things people want and need from the senior pastor to grow spiritually, we now have a dilemma. People *want* great preaching and vision casting—that's the category with the most dominant influence by far on satisfaction with the senior pastor—but people *need* spiritual challenge in order to grow. Our analysis showed that the ability to deliver spiritual challenge is the senior pastor's most influential driver of spiritual growth. Does that mean our hypothesis is correct? That people need spiritual challenge, but what they want is great preaching?

Not so fast. We need to address one additional question before we conclude that the data supports this hypothesis. That question is, If preaching and vision casting is what people want from the senior pastor, then what exactly do people want from preaching and vision casting? Just knowing that people want to hear a great sermon doesn't tell us what they want to get from that message.

The next step in our analysis is to dive more deeply into this very important preaching and vision-casting category to find answers. If this category is so critical to people's satisfaction with the senior pastor—in other words, if that's generally what makes them happy—then we need to be clear about precisely what they want.

WHAT DO PEOPLE WANT FROM PREACHING AND VISION CASTING?

To understand what people want from preaching and vision casting, we need to return to the statements we reviewed at the beginning of the chapter (chart 3-1, page 55). These are the statements used to determine the six categories of things people expect from the senior pastor. Now we're going to see which statements are most highly correlated with what congregants want from preaching and vision casting (chart 3-4).

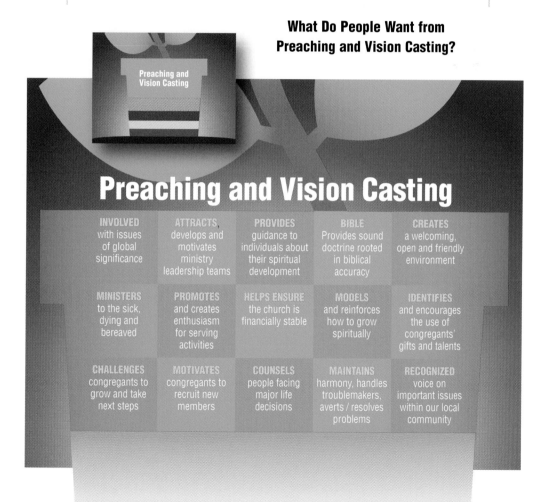

What Do People Want from Preaching and Vision Casting?

Preaching and Vision Casting

Preaching and Vision Casting

INVOLVED with issues of global significance	ATTRACTS, develops and motivates ministry leadership teams	PROVIDES guidance to individuals about their spiritual development	BIBLE Provides sound doctrine rooted in biblical accuracy	CREATES a welcoming, open and friendly environment
MINISTERS to the sick, dying and bereaved	PROMOTES and creates enthusiasm for serving activities	HELPS ENSURE the church is financially stable	MODELS and reinforces how to grow spiritually	IDENTIFIES and encourages the use of congregants' gifts and talents
CHALLENGES congregants to grow and take next steps	MOTIVATES congregants to recruit new members	COUNSELS people facing major life decisions	MAINTAINS harmony, handles troublemakers, averts / resolves problems	RECOGNIZED voice on important issues within our local community

Chart 3-4: This chart illustrates a shift in our analysis from the senior pastor to preaching and vision casting. The statements on the chart are the same statements we tested to identify the six categories of senior pastor responsibilities, one of which is preaching and vision casting. We used these same statements to determine what drives satisfaction with preaching and vision casting.

We found that three statements emerged as the most significant drivers of satisfaction with preaching and vision casting—and they were the same three statements that define the category of spiritual challenge. In other words, what people want from preaching and vision casting is spiritual challenge.

**The Three Characteristics That Define Spiritual Challenge
Consistently Drive Satisfaction with Preaching and Vision Casting**

Chart 3-5: The three statements at the top of this chart emerged as the characteristics that have the greatest impact on satisfaction with preaching and vision casting; they also define the spiritual challenge category. Although other statements also emerged as important to each of the four spiritual growth segments, it is the three statements defining spiritual challenge that consistently drive satisfaction with preaching and vision casting.

This holds true regardless of where a person is on the spiritual continuum. Chart 3-5 demonstrates that the three statements defining spiritual challenge are the same three statements that consistently drive satisfaction with preaching and vision casting for people in all four segments on the spiritual continuum.

We intentionally show the satisfaction drivers for each of the four segments on the spiritual continuum because we see big differences based on spiritual maturity. For example, the statement "promotes and creates enthusiasm for serving activities" is very influential for those who are in earlier stages of spiritual development (the Exploring Christ and Growing in Christ segments), but it's not influential for the more mature Close to Christ and Christ-Centered segments.

We see big differences based on spiritual maturity.

Out of all the statements we started with (chart 3-4, page 71), the ones shown for each segment on chart 3-5 emerged as the dominant drivers of satisfaction with preaching and vision casting. This means that the impact of the statements shown for each segment were head and shoulders above the rest. No other statements are included because their level of influence trails so far behind those on the chart. In sum, these are the statements that define what people want from preaching and vision casting for each segment on the spiritual continuum.

Based on what we discovered through this analysis, we offer five conclusions.

1. Spiritual challenge is what people want from preaching and vision casting.

Overall, the three statements that define spiritual challenge dominate what people want from preaching and vision casting. It's also worth noting that the statements are relatively equal in their level of influence for the three believer segments—Growing in Christ, Close to Christ and Christ-Centered. This means that biblical teaching, modeling spiritual growth and challenge are equally desired from preaching and vision casting by those who are followers of Christ.

The response of some to this conclusion might be, "Of course! What else would people want from an inspiring sermon besides spiritual challenge?" But others may be surprised and possibly even doubt that this conclusion is true for their congregations. We've met pastors who shy away from biblical challenge for fear of offending their congregants. We hope this finding is an encouragement to everyone who preaches God's Word—your congregants are hungry for as much spiritual challenge as you can deliver.

2. Sound doctrine and modeling influence everyone on the spiritual continuum.

Everyone strongly desires biblical teaching and modeling.

The statements "Provides sound doctrine rooted in biblical accuracy" and "Models and reinforces how to grow spiritually" are the only two that influence all four segments on the spiritual continuum. This means that everyone strongly desires biblical teaching and a senior pastor who models spiritual growth. If a senior pastor could do only two things incredibly well through preaching and vision casting, providing sound biblical doctrine and modeling spiritual growth are the two to focus on.

3. Challenge and next steps are important for all believers.

The statement "Challenges me to grow and take next steps" appears first in the Growing in Christ segment and continues to be a strong influence in the Close to Christ and Christ-Centered segments. A senior pastor's ability to challenge people to take their next steps to grow spiritually through preaching and vision casting is particularly important to those who have crossed the line of faith.

4. Serving is significant for those in the earlier segments of spiritual growth.

The statement "Promotes and creates enthusiasm for serving" shows up as a significant influence for those who are Exploring Christ and Growing in Christ. This means that people who are early in their spiritual development are especially receptive to messages that encourage serving, perhaps because they are looking for connection and community within the church. In addition, "creates a welcoming, open and friendly environment" is very influential for those who are Exploring Christ—again, a logical finding for those who are just beginning to explore Christianity.

The key here is that people are looking for these attributes to show up in the senior pastor's preaching and vision casting, which means they are looking to the senior pastor to set the tone for the values of the church.

5. Developing strong ministry leaders is important for those in the more mature segments of spiritual growth.

"Attracts, develops and motivates ministry leadership teams" is a statement of influence for those in the Close to Christ and Christ-Centered segments. While those who are less spiritually mature desire a welcoming environment and service opportunities, those who are more advanced spiritually want their senior pastor to develop leaders for ministry teams. This makes sense because those in the more mature segments are more likely to have experienced different ministry teams, and even been leaders themselves. Therefore, they would be more likely to appreciate the senior pastor's efforts to develop strong ministry leaders.

What people want most of all from the senior pastor is also exactly what they need.

We've covered a lot of territory about what people want and need from the senior pastor and what they want from preaching and vision casting in order to grow spiritually. We discovered that what people want from the senior pastor is preaching and vision casting; and we just reviewed findings that confirmed that what they want from preaching and vision casting is spiritual challenge. We also discovered that what people need most from their senior pastor to help them grow is spiritual challenge.

Therefore, we can conclude that what people want most of all from their senior pastor—spiritual challenge—is also exactly what they need from their senior pastor to help them grow spiritually (chart 3-6). Spiritual challenge is the senior pastor's biggest driver of both spiritual growth and satisfaction.

This conclusion begs the question, Does the senior pastor deliver spiritual challenge *only* through preaching and vision casting? In other words, if the senior pastor delivers a compelling spiritual challenge through a message at the weekend service, is that all that's required to catalyze spiritual growth in the congregation?

Spiritual Challenge Is What People Want and Need from the Senior Pastor

Chart 3-6: Preaching and vision casting drive satisfaction with the senior pastor, and spiritual challenge drives satisfaction with preaching and vision casting. This means spiritual challenge is the underlying force with the greatest impact on people's satisfaction with the senior pastor. It is also through spiritual challenge that the senior pastor has the greatest influence on spiritual growth. These two analyses—the first about the most influential drivers of satisfaction with the senior pastor's preaching and vision casting and the second about the senior pastor's greatest influence on spiritual growth—independently reach the same conclusion. Spiritual challenge is what people want and need most from the senior pastor for spiritual growth.

The activities of the senior pastor between services are devoted largely to leading the church. Does the need for the senior pastor to provide spiritual challenge extend beyond weekend preaching and vision casting to this day-to-day leadership role? If so, how does that work? And does anyone in the church care? These are the questions that led us to develop our final hypothesis: *What people need from the church is spiritual guidance and what they need from the senior pastor is spiritual challenge, but what they want is a great weekend service.*

What about leadership?

This hypothesis reflects our assumption that preaching and vision casting at weekend services is the senior pastor's role with the greatest influence on satisfaction with the church. That's why our hypothesis says a great weekend service is what people really want. The implication is that the senior pastor's role as leader of the church is much less important to people than the role of preaching and vision casting.

DO PEOPLE CARE ABOUT LEADERSHIP—OR JUST GREAT WEEKEND SERVICES?

We begin this final analysis by returning to the lists of top priorities for the church and senior pastor (chart 3-7, page 78). At this point, we have reduced thirty-three statements about what people want and need from the church and from the senior pastor to a combined top-ten list—seven statements about spiritual guidance for the church and three statements about spiritual challenge for the senior pastor. You'll notice that one statement appears twice. "Challenges me to grow and take next steps" shows up on the list of what people want and need from both the church and the senior pastor. Although the statements are the same, they represent two distinct priorities because they relate to two distinct senior pastor roles—teaching and leading the church.

The Top Ten Things People Want and Need from the Church and the Senior Pastor

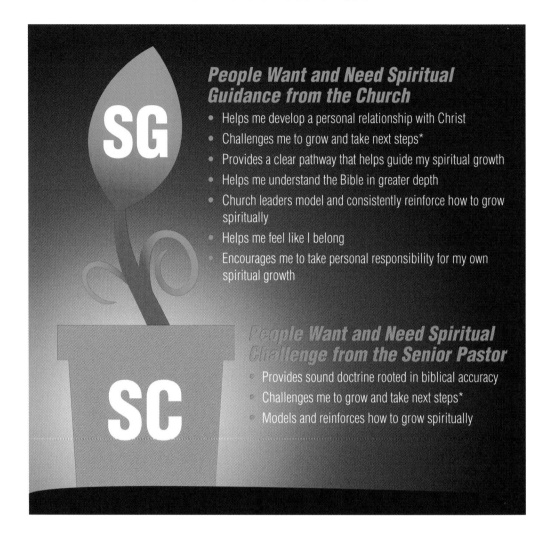

People Want and Need Spiritual Guidance from the Church

SG

- Helps me develop a personal relationship with Christ
- Challenges me to grow and take next steps*
- Provides a clear pathway that helps guide my spiritual growth
- Helps me understand the Bible in greater depth
- Church leaders model and consistently reinforce how to grow spiritually
- Helps me feel like I belong
- Encourages me to take personal responsibility for my own spiritual growth

People Want and Need Spiritual Challenge from the Senior Pastor

SC

- Provides sound doctrine rooted in biblical accuracy
- Challenges me to grow and take next steps*
- Models and reinforces how to grow spiritually

Chart 3-7: These ten statements represent the essential qualities people want and need from senior pastors and churches to help them grow spiritually.

*"Challenges me to grow and take next steps" shows up on the list of what people want and need from both the church and the senior pastor. Although the statements are the same, they represent two distinct priorities because they relate to two distinct senior pastor roles—teaching and leading the church.

Now we are going to take a closer look at these two roles in order to determine which role has the greatest impact on spiritual growth.

We began our work by making one key assumption: Everything starts with the senior pastor. We made that assumption because the senior pastor's influence is pervasive—not only through the preaching and vision-casting role at weekend services, but also through the role of leading the church.

Chart 3-8 (page 80) illustrates how we tried to determine which role—teaching or leading—was most influential to spiritual growth.[11] We started with the senior pastor at the top of the chart and analyzed the influence of the senior pastor's teaching and leading on satisfaction with the church's role in spiritual growth. In other words, assuming satisfaction with the church is a proxy for the church's effectiveness in helping people grow spiritually, we wanted to know which role—teacher or leader—had the greatest impact on satisfaction, and consequently on spiritual growth.

We wanted to know which role had the greatest impact.

Our goal was to compare the importance of teaching to the importance of leading on satisfaction with the church, and thus spiritual growth. Why? Because if teaching is much more important to spiritual growth than leadership, then the bulk of the senior pastor's time should be spent preparing to teach. But if leading the church is the more essential role, then that would have different implications for the best use of the senior pastor's time and energy.

The arrow on the left side of chart 3-8 illustrates the senior pastor's ability to deliver spiritual challenge through preaching and vision casting, which typically takes place at the weekend services. We expected that this would be a powerful avenue of influence.

The arrow on the right side of the chart depicts the senior pastor's ability to deliver spiritual challenge through leading the church. We evaluated the role of leading the church in a very special way. We looked specifically at the senior pastor's impact on the church through all the factors related to spiritual guidance. This means we looked at the senior pastor's impact on creating a church that helps people understand the Bible in depth; provides challenge and next steps; has leaders that model spiritual growth and so on. Basically, this

[11] For more information about the methodology used in this analysis, see "A Note about the Analysis of the Senior Pastor's Impact Through Preaching and Through Leading the Church" on pages 111–12.

The Senior Pastor Delivers Spiritual Challenge through
Two Roles: Teaching and Leading

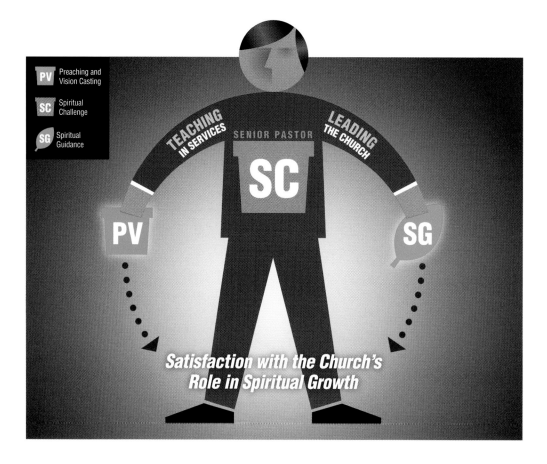

Chart 3-8: This chart depicts two ways the senior pastor's delivery of spiritual challenge impacts people's satisfaction with the church—teaching and leading. Preaching and vision casting at weekend services is the senior pastor's most visible and vocal platform for spiritual challenge. But delivering spiritual challenge through leadership—by creating a church in which spiritual guidance flourishes—is also a role of great influence.

reflects the senior pastor's impact on satisfaction with the church through everything except preaching and vision casting.

We expected to find that the senior pastor's most influential role would be teaching at the weekend service. In fact, we expected teaching to be significantly more influential than leading the church. But what we actually found surprised us. And that's an understatement.

We discovered that the role of leading the church had four times the impact on satisfaction with the church's role in spiritual growth compared to the role of teaching (chart 3-9). Specifically, the role of teaching accounted for 20 percent of the senior pastor's influence on satisfaction with the church's role in spiritual growth, and the role of leading accounted for 80 percent. In other words, the senior pastor's leadership of the church—which means making and executing the

Leading accounts for 80 percent of the senior pastor's impact.

The Senior Pastor's Leadership Role Has the Greatest Impact on Satisfaction with the Church's Role in Spiritual Growth

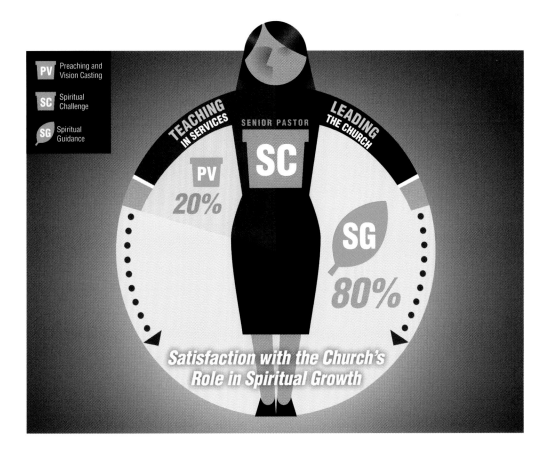

Chart 3-9: This chart demonstrates the much greater influence of the senior pastor's leadership role, relative to the senior pastor's teaching role, on satisfaction with how well the church helps people grow spiritually.

kinds of decisions that create an environment of spiritual challenge and spiritual guidance in all ministries—drives satisfaction with the church's role in spiritual growth by a margin of four to one. Interestingly, we also found that weekend services have little to no influence on satisfaction with the church independent of the influence of preaching and vision casting.

What does this mean?

Your people appreciate your leadership.

This finding implies that even the best sermon doesn't have nearly the impact as do the day-to-day decisions a senior pastor makes about how to lead a church—specifically the decisions that deliver spiritual guidance through the church. For example, decisions about which job candidate to hire based in part on which one is likely to serve as the best role model. Decisions about starting new ministries or discontinuing old ones based on the ministry's ability to help people grow spiritually. Decisions about which compassion-related causes to undertake based on the capacity of each cause to challenge the congregation spiritually. These are the kind of choices and tough calls that reflect a senior pastor's values and reverberate throughout the church and its community long after weekend services have come and gone.

Our encouragement to senior pastors is that your people appreciate all the choices you face and the tough calls you make. Beyond your teaching at weekend services, they appreciate your leadership much more than you might have imagined.

This finding also shows that the spiritual growth of your congregation depends on having a senior pastor who does two things: (1) delivers spiritual challenge through both teaching and leading; (2) demonstrates through daily decisions and behaviors that the role of leadership is the one deserving the senior pastor's greatest time, energy and attention.

FROM HYPOTHESES TO DECLARATIONS

In this chapter we've wrestled with two hypotheses about what people want and need from the senior pastor in order to grow spiritually:

- What people need from the senior pastor is spiritual challenge, but what they want is great preaching.

- What people need is spiritual guidance from the church and spiritual challenge from the senior pastor, but what they want is a great weekend service.

We acknowledged earlier that the responsibilities of a senior pastor are wide ranging and complex. Our objective was to determine whether or not some of those responsibilities, like preaching and vision casting, were worthy of more time and energy than others because they have greater impact on spiritual growth. We also wanted to confirm or dispel the notion that what people want from the senior pastor is different than what they need to grow spiritually. I'll close this chapter by reviewing our conclusions.

Spiritual Challenge Versus Great Preaching

We confirmed that, in fact, what people need from their senior pastor is spiritual challenge, but what they want is great preaching. Then we went a step further to determine what people want from great preaching. The answer was spiritual challenge.

Now we can modify our first hypothesis and offer this declaration: *People want and need spiritual challenge from the senior pastor.*

This means that what people want and need from their senior pastor boils down to these three statements:

People want and need spiritual challenge from the senior pastor.

- Provides sound doctrine rooted in biblical accuracy
- Challenges people to grow and take next steps
- Models and reinforces how to grow spiritually

Based on our findings, senior pastors who use these statements as the organizing framework for their preaching and vision casting—and their daily ministry decisions—can be confident that what they are doing will help their people to grow spiritually.

Spiritual Challenge and Guidance Versus a Great Weekend Service

Our final hypothesis was that people need spiritual guidance from the church and spiritual challenge from the senior pastor, but what they want is a great weekend service. But we discovered that what people need and want most of all from the senior pastor is great leadership.

Choose to lead.

The senior pastor's most important role is to create a church culture and environment that delivers the seven requirements of spiritual guidance. This is the kind of church that challenges people to develop a personal relationship with Christ; provides them with a clear pathway of spiritual growth and encourages them to pursue it; helps people understand the Bible in greater depth; develops leaders who are spiritual role models; and helps people feel like they belong. Creating this kind of church is the ultimate outcome of a senior pastor who delivers spiritual challenge.

This leads to our third and final declaration: *People want and need spiritual challenge from their senior pastor, and they want and need spiritual guidance from their church—but what they want and need most of all is great leadership.*

Based on this research, if a senior pastor has to choose between being a great teacher or a great leader, the choice is clear.

Choose to lead.

GREG L. HAWKINS

FOCUS

4

GIVE THEM WHAT THEY WANT

big picture

WHEN ALL IS SAID AND DONE, we need to know the bottom line. Here we look at the big-picture implications and practical applications of our research, summing it all up in two power-packed sentences.

4

GIVE THEM WHAT THEY WANT

When I am invited to speak to other pastors and share what we are learning from REVEAL research, I almost always get the same questions: "Can you net it out for us? What's the bottom line?" Pastors want to know, in very practical terms, what all these findings mean for the way they lead their churches.

I understand completely, and I wrestle with these same questions myself. I'm a systems thinker, and I enjoy taking a lot of complex information and trying to make sense of it. I like the intellectual challenge, but I am also ruthlessly pragmatic. If what I discover does not help me or someone else to be more effective in their work or life, it's worthless information.

"What's the bottom line?"

Over the past few years, I have wrestled with the findings from each new round of REVEAL research, trying to understand both the big-picture implications and the practical applications—for my own church and for the churches who are learning along with us. In light of our latest findings and our experience at Willow Creek, I want to give you the bottom line in two sentences that summarize the statements on our top-ten list. Then I will unpack each sentence with some practical suggestions. Here are the two sentences:

> As church leaders, we need to give people a place to belong and a pathway that guides them on their journey toward intimacy with Christ. We catalyze their spiritual growth by helping them understand the Bible in greater depth, by challenging them to apply the Scriptures with specific next steps and by modeling how we are taking those steps ourselves.

Let's take a closer look at each of these sentences and consider how we can apply these principles to our own churches.

> ## As church leaders, we need to give people a place to belong and a pathway that guides them on their journey toward intimacy with Christ.

I know it's a mouthful, but this sentence has four important parts that we need to unpack one at a time.

A place to belong

Belonging does not mean that people are connected in a small group or in a serving role. As Cally mentioned in chapter 2, belonging is about people wanting to know if they fit in at your church. And they make that decision very early—within the first several weeks or months of attending services. So help them out. Let them know what you believe, what you are trying to accomplish, what you expect from them and what they can expect from you. Make it very clear so they can opt in or out early on. You can put this in writing or on your web site, but several churches who do this well host a class or gathering and strongly encourage newcomers to attend.

Church leaders are coaches who show people the way.

A pathway

We need to give people a pathway that leads them in their spiritual journey. Church leaders are coaches who show people the way. As the Home Depot slogan goes, "You can do it. We can help." That should be our motto as well. Like a good coach, we need to point the way. We must tell people who are early in the journey what their first steps are. As they advance, we must help them understand what comes next.

In studying several particularly effective churches, we hoped we might find one great pathway that every church could use. We didn't find anything like that, but every effective church we studied did have

The (Top Ten Things) People Want and Need from the Church and the Senior Pastor*

People Want and Need Spiritual Guidance from the Church

- Helps me develop a personal relationship with Christ
- Challenges me to grow and take next steps**
- Provides a clear pathway that helps guide my spiritual growth
- Helps me understand the Bible in greater depths
- Church leaders model and consistently reinforce how to grow spiritually
- Helps me feel like I belong
- Encourages me to take responsibility for my own growth

People Want and Need Spiritual Challenge from the Senior Pastor

- Provides sound doctrine rooted in biblical accuracy
- Challenges me to grow and take next steps**
- Models and reinforces how to grow spiritually ◆

* Statements are listed in random order.

** "Challenges me to grow and take next steps" shows up on the list of what people want and need from both the church and the senior pastor. Although the statements are the same, they represent two distinct priorities because they relate to two distinct senior pastor roles—teaching and leading the church.

---

a pathway around which they aligned their activities. Our takeaway is that it's not how great the pathway is, but how effectively the pathway is implemented that is the real key.

Their journey

From the beginning, we need to let congregants know that participation in the church is about their spiritual journey toward a deeper relationship with God—a journey they must own for themselves. They must understand that we are there to help and to encourage their growth, but ultimately they must choose to be responsible. As Bill Hybels has repeatedly told our church, "I can't read your Bible for you." We must instill a sense of personal responsibility in the people we lead and serve.

"I can't read your Bible for you."

Intimacy with Christ

Our people must understand that the goal of this journey is a deep, intimate relationship with Christ. A relationship that is so important that they freely choose to surrender and resurrender their agenda and will to God's agenda for them and this world. As my friend Jimmy Knott from First Baptist of Orlando says, "I am not here to make you a better Baptist. I am here to make you a disciple of Jesus Christ." Crystal clear.

Think of the four components of this first sentence as the things that create the environment and conditions for spiritual growth to occur. If we do our jobs right, people will have a strong sense of belonging, will know where they are headed, will have a clear path to guide their steps and will be motivated to take personal responsibility for their journey toward intimacy with Christ. All the essential conditions are in place. Now we just need something to catalyze their growth. That is what the second sentence is all about.

> **We catalyze their spiritual growth by helping them understand the Bible in greater depth, by challenging them to apply the Scriptures with specific next steps and by modeling how we are taking those steps ourselves.**

People should walk away feeling like their minds and hearts were expanded.

Here we have three prominent themes: Bible, challenge and modeling. I want to address each one briefly and then show you how they work together to produce tremendous spiritual growth.

Bible
The first component is biblical teaching that is rooted in sound doctrine and increases people's understanding of Scripture. Every time God's Word is taught, people should walk away feeling like their minds and hearts were expanded. They should be thinking things like "I never knew that before" or "I understand that passage so much better now."

Challenge

Using the words of Scripture, we need to challenge people to apply these truths to their lives in very tangible ways. The key is to link the challenge with the Scripture. That is what gives your challenge authority. A challenge that is not linked to God's Word will not bear fruit. And make sure the challenge always has concrete action steps for people to take.

Modeling

We must be transparent enough to show people how we live out biblical principles in our own lives. We can teach the Bible and challenge people, but if they don't hear and see us living this out, they won't be inclined to do it themselves.

We must show people how we live out biblical principles.

Here's an example of how Bible, challenge and modeling can work together in powerful ways. At the beginning of a three-week emphasis on global poverty, one of our teaching pastors, Darren Whitehead, taught on Jesus' parable of the Good Samaritan (Luke 10:25–37). He explained what this particular stretch of road would have been like two thousand years ago; he unpacked the deeply held biases that would have made the priest and Levite pass by the wounded man on the other side of the road; and he helped us all understand the full cost the Good Samaritan paid to provide assistance.

Darren then helped us apply what we'd learned to our own lives with a punch line about what it really means to bear someone else's burden: "To bear a burden, you must share the burden. If it doesn't cost you something—time, attention, money—you have not helped lift their burden." Bearing another person's burdens has to cost us something.

Bill Hybels followed the teaching with three direct challenges and concrete next steps. First, he asked us to restrict our diet for the next five days to eat as the poorest half of the world's population eats every day: oatmeal for breakfast, beans and rice for lunch and dinner. By doing so we would identify with the poor and open ourselves to God to tell us other ways we could help. Second, he challenged everyone to spend two hours within the next few weeks to help pack meals for children in Zimbabwe. As a church we were packing four million meals, and we needed everyone to help. Third, he asked us to pray about making a financial gift to alleviate poverty in Africa.

Bill modeled his own commitment by sharing his experience of a similar food challenge the church did last year and how it changed him. He talked about how he felt on each of the five days. He mentioned that on day five he realized that the challenge would soon be over for him and he could go back to eating whatever he wanted, but the poor had no such option. It was clear he took this teaching seriously, and it made the rest of us wonder why we wouldn't want to do the same.

All three elements—Bible, challenge and modeling—are essential all the time.

The response from our congregation was amazing. Thousands participated in the restricted diet, over 17,500 people served a two-hour shift packing meals and at the end of three weeks we collected over $1.9 million to provide food and clean water for impoverished communities in Africa. I don't have proof, but I also believe the spiritual temperature in our church went up as a result. The key was linking the challenge to teaching from God's Word, and offering specific next steps for people to take.

My very strong belief is that all three elements—Bible, challenge and modeling—are essential all the time. When you teach God's Word and challenge people with it, always follow up by suggesting the practical next steps they can take. And demonstrate how you are taking that step. If you take out any of the three elements, you are missing out on an opportunity to really help people grow.

JESUS LED THIS WAY

Here I must state the obvious: Jesus did *everything* on the top-ten list. And he did it perfectly. If you want to know how to put these ten into action, just read the gospels.

Jesus helped everyone feel like they belonged—men and women, Jews and Gentiles, adults and children; and he clearly defined the path people should take to grow closer to God. "I am the way and the truth and the life. No one comes to the Father except through me" (John 14:6). He made it clear that he himself was the path, and his invitation to those he met was, "Follow me."

Jesus taught the Scriptures and helped everyone understand them in more depth. "When Jesus had finished saying these things, the crowds were amazed at his teaching, because he taught as one who had authority" (Matthew 7:28, 29a).

He challenged people to grow and take next steps. He was never content to let people stay where they were spiritually. He consistently pointed out the next step for each person he encountered. When the rich young ruler asked Jesus, "What good thing must I do to get eternal life?" Jesus responded, "If you want to be perfect, go, sell your possessions and give to the poor, and you will have treasure in heaven. Then come, follow me" (Matthew 19:16, 21).

And Jesus constantly modeled how to grow closer to God. For example, he not only taught the disciples about prayer—"This, then, is how you should pray: Our Father . . ." (Matthew 6:9)—he also reinforced his teaching by letting the disciples see how he prayed, including his struggling prayers in the Garden of Gethsemane.

This is how Jesus led and how he catalyzed growth in those who followed him.

ONE MORE THING

I believe you really want to help your people grow. You care deeply about their needs, and you are open to hearing about what they want. I know this is true because living out the calling to lead and pastor others is hard work—no one chooses this task lightly. You do it because you really do want to make more and better disciples of Christ.

Because we have such a desire to see people grow, it can be hard for us to stay focused on the essential things we must do, especially when we

It can be hard for us to stay focused on the essential things we must do.

are constantly bombarded with so many needs (and wants). It is hard to know who to say yes to and who to say no to. It is hard to know which ministries to start and which ones to shut down. It is hard figuring out what to preach Sunday after Sunday.

I believe the top-ten list can help us all make better decisions. In fact, the REVEAL insights have significantly improved our ministry here at Willow. Recently, we resurveyed our congregation and found strong evidence that acting on what we've learned from REVEAL has fostered greater levels of spiritual growth in our congregation.

But maybe all the data analysis and empirical results haven't convinced you to embrace our conclusions. If so, maybe the words of Jesus will convince you. In the Great Commission (Matthew 28:16–20), Jesus clearly directs us to "go make disciples," but he doesn't stop there. Here's the part of that commission that gets a bit less airtime: "Teach them to obey everything I have commanded you."

Are you willing to focus on what's most important?

I need to confess that for many years that phrase "obey everything" sure felt heavy and oppressive. But recently, because of this research, I have come to see it differently. As a pastor, I understand that Jesus is telling me to (a) make sure people know what he commanded (teach the Bible in greater depth); and (b) call them to fully live out his commands (challenge and point out next steps).

Why does Jesus want us to do these things? Because as we conform our lives to the truth of his Word, we grow closer to him. "If you obey my commands, you will remain in my love, just as I have obeyed my Father's commands and remain in his love" (John 15:10). He loves us and he knows what we need. We might not want to obey, but we really need to in order to experience the fullness of life that Jesus promises.

Pastors and leaders, it's up to you. Are you willing to focus on what's most important and give people what they really need? It's not as hard as it might sound. You already have one thing going for you. What they need *is* what they want.

Give them what they want.

APPENDICES

DO WANTS AND NEEDS CHANGE DEPENDING ON THE SIZE OF THE CHURCH?

NANCY K. SCAMMACCA, Ph. D.

DO PEOPLE WHO ATTEND larger churches want and need different things from the church and the senior pastor in order to grow spiritually? Conventional wisdom suggests the answer is yes, but we wanted to take a closer look at the issue from the perspective of our database of 376 churches of varying sizes.

We divided the churches in our database into four groups based on current weekend adult attendance (chart A1-1).

Chart A1-1

Attendance Levels in the 376 Churches

Size of Church	Number of Churches	Number of Respondents
250 or less	139	11,842
251–999	191	43,862
1000–2499	37	18,112
2500 or more	9	6047
TOTAL	**376**	**79,863**

Although our database is quite large, most (88 percent) of the churches we surveyed have an average weekly adult attendance below 1,000. Just nine of the 376 churches in our database (2 percent) have a weekly attendance of 2,500 or more. It isn't surprising that we had so few very large churches, given that these churches represent a small percentage of all churches in America. However, it is important to keep in mind that our results might have been different if we had been able to include more very large churches in the survey.

The Impact of Church Size on Expectations of the Church

When we looked at what people want from the church to help them grow spiritually, we found no differences based on the size of the church. Spiritual guidance and belonging came out on top in every group, and the importance of each factor to satisfaction with the church's role in spiritual growth was similar.

When it comes to what people need from the church to grow spiritually, we did see some differences based on the size of the church. However, we found differences only in the group of churches

Chart A1-2

In Very Large Churches, Accountability/Impact and Serving Are the Most Influential Catalysts of Spiritual Growth for Movement 1: Exploring Christ to Growing in Christ

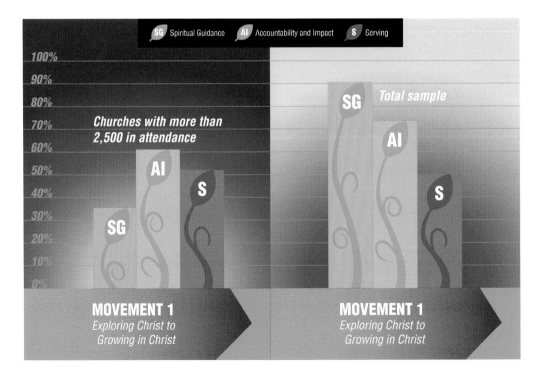

with attendance of 2,500 or more. In the movement from Exploring Christ to Growing in Christ, accountability/impact and serving were most catalytic to growth for people who attend very large churches. Spiritual guidance was the third-most-important factor, but its influence was much smaller for those in very large churches than it was for those in other churches (chart A1-2).

Accountability/impact and spiritual guidance remained the most important catalysts of spiritual growth in the movement from Growing in Christ to Close to Christ across all sizes of churches. But in the movement from Close to Christ to Christ-Centered, the influence of serving was as large as accountability and impact for those attending churches of 2,500 or more. Spiritual guidance was somewhat less important to growth for those attending very large churches than for others (chart A1-3).

Chart A1-3

In Very Large Churches, Serving Is the Most Influential Catalyst of Spiritual Growth for Movement 3: Close to Christ to Christ-Centered

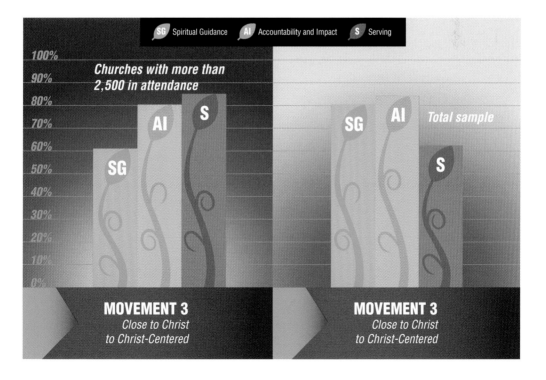

Our findings indicate that if church size does matter, it is only for the very largest churches. In these churches, serving those in need has a greater catalytic effect on spiritual growth than is seen in smaller churches. One reason for this effect may be that larger churches can offer a broader range of serving opportunities and can support ministries to those in need more easily than smaller churches. More opportunities likely translate into greater involvement in serving for those who attend these churches. But again, it's important to remember that only nine churches in our database were in this group of churches, so our findings need to be tested with more very large churches before we can draw definitive conclusions.

The Impact of Church Size on Expectations of the Senior Pastor

It seems reasonable that any organization of 250 people would require different qualities and priorities in its leader than an organization of 1,000 or 2,500 people. Many church growth books encourage senior pastors to shift their role in the church as the church grows. We looked at our data by church size to see if church size affected what people want and need from their senior pastor.

In the previous section, we noted that there were no differences in what people want from the church based on church size. The results are the same when it comes to what people want from their senior pastor—there are no differences based on church size. Preaching and vision casting came out on top for each group of churches, and its impact on satisfaction with the senior pastor was similar.

When we looked at what people need from their senior pastor to grow, we found differences in needs only for those in the very largest churches. In the movement from Exploring Christ to Growing in Christ, pastoral care was the most catalytic factor for people in churches of 2,500 or more. This finding is surprising, given that the impact of pastoral care in every other group of churches was close to zero (which led us to drop this factor from the results reported in chapter 3). In the movements from Growing in Christ to Close to Christ and from Close to Christ to Christ-Centered, spiritual challenge was the greatest catalyst across all churches, no matter the size.

Based on these results, it appears that people who are just beginning their faith journey in very large churches may have a particular need for individual guidance and counseling from the senior pastor. Again, however, we are cautious in making too much of our findings given that just nine churches of 2,500 or more participated in this phase of our research.

So Does Church Size Matter?

Our results indicate that the size of the church makes very little difference in what people need and want from their church and senior pastor to help them grow spiritually. We found differences only in churches with a weekly adult attendance of 2,500 or more. Serving appears to play a larger role in spiritual growth for people who attend these churches than it does for those who attend smaller churches. Also, people who are in the initial stage of spiritual growth in very large churches seem to have a particular need for pastoral care from their senior pastor to catalyze their growth. Because our database contained just nine churches with attendance of 2,500 or more, we need to collect data from more very large churches before we can have complete confidence that size does make a difference for people in these churches.

Nancy K. Scammacca holds a Ph.D. in quantitative methods from the University of Texas. In addition to her consulting work with REVEAL, she serves part time on the pastoral staff of MESA Community Church in Austin, Texas, and consults on research projects in education and the social sciences.

WHAT IS REVEAL?

A Research-Based View of the Spiritual Journey

REVEAL is a research-based view of how the spiritual journey unfolds, validated to date through survey input from over 235,000 congregants in more than 850 churches.[1] The distinction of REVEAL is its ability to "measure the unseen," using a research approach that assesses how people's spiritual attitudes, needs and motivations align with spiritual behaviors.

REVEAL identifies a spiritual continuum comprised of four segments of people at different stages of spiritual development: Exploring Christ, Growing in Christ, Close to Christ and Christ-Centered. REVEAL's deeper value, however, is found in its insights about what creates movement along the journey; for example, which church activities, beliefs, spiritual practices or activities (evangelism, serving, etc.) are most influential to spiritual growth at different points along the journey.

Three Books

Published in 2007, *Reveal: Where Are You?* describes the initial aggregate findings based on input from 5,000 surveys completed by seven different congregations.

---

[1] For more information and a brief history of REVEAL, visit www.revealnow.com.

A second book, *Follow Me: What's Next for You?* published in 2008, expands on earlier findings about the four segments on the spiritual continuum by describing the spiritual catalysts most influential to movement along the continuum. The findings in *Follow Me* are based on input from 80,000 surveys completed by people in more than 200 congregations in October and November 2007.

Focus: The Top Ten Things People Want and Need from You and Your Church compares the drivers of satisfaction with the church and senior pastor (what people want) with the most influential catalysts of spiritual growth (what people need). Its findings are based on input from 80,000 people in 376 churches who participated in the REVEAL Spiritual Life Survey between September 2008 and February 2009.

A Spiritual Life Survey

The Spiritual Life Survey is a research tool local churches can use to assess the spiritual health of their congregations. The goal of the Spiritual Life Survey is to provide church leaders with a research tool equivalent to the finest research tool used in the marketplace at a small fraction of the marketplace cost. For more information, see Appendix 5, "What Is the REVEAL Spiritual Life Survey?" (page 117), or visit www.revealnow.com.

RESEARCH APPROACH AND METHODOLOGY

REVEAL began with a simple question: Could scientific research help us understand and perhaps measure spiritual growth? In other words, could the same research tools used in the marketplace to measure consumer attitudes and behaviors also be used by local churches to measure the spiritual beliefs and behaviors of their congregations? We believed the answer was yes.

We have refined our research over the course of four years, more than 850 churches and 235,000 individual surveys. While we're still in the early phases of our work, we feel confident that the research survey tool and analyses have proven capable of producing valid and valuable insight for church leaders.

Here is a brief overview of our research approach and methodology.

Approach

Our approach focused on three key areas and questions related to those areas:

- **Segments:** What are the different groups/segments of people the church might be looking to serve?
- **Needs:** What spiritual growth needs are being met, not being met well or not being met at all for each segment?
- **Drivers and Barriers:** What are the drivers of spiritual growth, and what are the barriers to spiritual growth?

These three areas provided the framework around which we organized the information we collected.

Methodology

Broadly speaking, there are two types of research methodology: qualitative and quantitative. We used both qualitative and quantitative methodologies, and then employed analytical techniques and processes to review the data.

Qualitative (Gathering Insights)

This is typically a one-on-one process in which a researcher poses questions directly to an individual. The questions often ask not only for information and opinions but also allow the interviewer to probe the richness of emotions and motivations related to the topic. Researchers use qualitative data to help clarify hypotheses, beliefs, attitudes and motivations. Qualitative work is often a first step because it enables a researcher to fine-tune the language that will be used in quantitative tools.

Quantitative (Establishing Statistical Reliability and Validity)

This process utilizes detailed questionnaires often distributed to large numbers of people. Questions are typically multiple choice, and participants choose the most appropriate response among those listed for each question. Quantitative research collects a huge amount of data, which can often be generalized to a larger population and allow for direct comparisons between two or more groups. It also provides statisticians with several options for methods to use in analyzing the results.

Analytical Process and Techniques (Quantifying Insights and Conclusions)

Quantitative research involves an analytical plan designed to process the data to yield empirically based insights. Several analytical techniques were used in our four research phases:

- **Correlation Analysis:** Measures the extent to which two variables are related (if at all). Finding a correlation does not mean that one variable causes the other; it means their patterns of movement are connected.
- **Discriminant Analysis:** Determines which variables best explain the differences between two or more groups. We can't infer that these variables directly cause the differences to occur between the groups. Instead, we know that there are significant differences between the groups on the variables.
- **Regression Analysis:** Used to investigate relationships between variables. This technique is typically utilized to determine whether or not the movement of an outcome (or dependent) variable can be predicted from one or more independent variables.

- **Hierarchical Cluster Analysis:** Used to determine which survey items are most similar to each other in their statistical properties and group them accordingly. This analysis was conducted on half of our dataset to group into categories items that measured the ways the church and the senior pastor help people grow spiritually. The validity of the grouping could then be tested using confirmatory factor analysis.

- **Confirmatory Factor Analysis:** Used to test a model that theorizes that a group of items on a survey measure one or more shared underlying constructs. The model is tested to determine how well the data fit the theory. Good fit validates the theory. This analysis was conducted on the second half of our dataset to validate the grouping into categories of items that measured the ways the church and the senior pastor help people grow spiritually—five categories for the church and six for the senior pastor.

- **Path Analysis:** An advanced technique related to regression analysis used to determine the relative effect of multiple variables on an outcome (or dependent) variable. Indirect effects (where the effect of one or more variables on the outcome variable is mediated by another variable) can be calculated. A theoretical model of direct and indirect effects is developed and tested to determine how well the data fit the theory. Acceptable fit validates the theory. Path analysis was conducted to determine the senior pastor's effect on satisfaction with the church's role in spiritual growth through preaching versus through leadership of the church.

We used both qualitative and quantitative methods in 2004 when we focused exclusively on Willow Creek Community Church and also in our 2007–2009 research involving hundreds of churches. Here is a summary of the methodology used in our most recent work.

Qualitative Phase (December 2006)

- *One-on-one interviews with sixty-eight congregants.* We specifically recruited people in the more advanced stages of spiritual growth. Our goal was to capture language and insights to help guide the development of our survey questionnaire.

- *Interview duration:* 30–45 minutes

- *Focused on fifteen topics.* Topics included spiritual life history, church background, personal spiritual practices, spiritual attitudes and beliefs, etc.

Quantitative Phases

PHASE 1 (January–February 2007)

- E-mail survey fielded with seven churches diverse in geography, size, ethnicity and format

- Received 4,943 completed surveys

- Utilized fifty-three sets of questions on topics such as:
  - ✦ Attitudes about Christianity and one's personal spiritual life
  - ✦ Personal spiritual practices, including statements about frequency of Bible reading, prayer, journaling, etc.
  - ✦ Satisfaction with the role of the church in spiritual growth
  - ✦ Importance and satisfaction of specific church attributes (e.g., helps me understand the Bible in depth) related to spiritual growth
  - ✦ Most significant barriers to spiritual growth
  - ✦ Participation and satisfaction with church activities, such as weekend services, small groups, youth ministries and serving

PHASE 2 (April–May 2007)

- E-mail survey fielded with twenty-five churches diverse in geography, size, ethnicity and format

- Received 15,977 completed surveys

- Utilized a refined set of questions based on Phase 1 research

PHASE 3 (October–November 2007 and January–February 2008)

- E-mail survey fielded with 487 churches diverse in geography, size, ethnicity and format, including ninety-one churches in seventeen countries

- Received 136,547 completed surveys

- Utilized a refined set of questions based on Phase 2 research
  - ✦ Expanded survey to include twenty statements about core Christian beliefs and practices from *The Christian Life Profile Assessment Tool Training Kit.*[1]

---

[1] Randy Frazee, *The Christian Life Profile Assessment Tool Training Kit* (Grand Rapids, Mich.: Zondervan, 2005).

✤ Added importance and satisfaction measures for specific attributes related to weekend services, small groups, children's and youth ministries and serving experiences.

PHASE 4 (September 2008–March 2009)

- E-mail survey fielded with 376 churches diverse in geography, size, ethnicity and format

- Received 79,863 completed surveys

- Utilized a refined set of questions based on Phase 3 research and qualitative data from interviews with best-practice churches

  ✤ Expanded survey to include seventeen items measuring importance and satisfaction with aspects of the senior pastor's leadership
  ✤ Added eight items measuring importance and satisfaction with aspects of the church's role in spiritual growth

Analytical Process and Resources

Each phase of our research included an analytical plan executed by statisticians and research professionals. These plans utilized many analytical techniques, including correlation, regression, discriminant analysis, cluster analysis, confirmatory factor analysis and path analysis. In *Focus*, our findings about what people need from the church and the senior pastor are derived primarily from extensive discriminant analysis. Our findings about what people want from the church and senior pastor are derived primarily from extensive regression analyses. To put our analytical approach into perspective, here are three points of explanation about the nature of our research philosophy.

1. Our research is a snapshot in time.

Because this research is intentionally done at one point in time—like a snapshot—it is impossible to determine with certainty that a given variable, such as valuing spiritual guidance from the church, causes movement from one segment to another (for example, from Growing in Christ to Close to Christ). To establish causality, we would have to assess the spiritual development of the same people over a period of time (longitudinal research).

However, the fact that increased levels of valuing spiritual guidance occur in the Close to Christ segment compared with the Growing in Christ segment strongly suggests that valuing spiritual guidance from the church does influence spiritual movement between segments. While it does not determine conclusively that spiritual guidance "causes" movement, discriminant analysis does identify the most differentiating characteristics between segments. So we infer from the findings that certain factors are more "predictive" and consequently more influential to spiritual growth than others.

Our ultimate goal is to measure the same people over multiple points in time (longitudinal research) in order to more clearly understand the causal effects of spiritual growth. Longitudinal research is challenging to conduct because it involves tracking people as they move or change churches over time. It is usually undertaken after "snapshot" research has identified the key variables to focus on measuring long term. However, even with longitudinal findings, we know there will be much left to learn, and much we will never understand about spiritual formation. The attitudes and behaviors we measure today should not be misinterpreted as defining spiritual formation. Instead they should be considered instruments used by the Holy Spirit to open our hearts for God's formative work.

2. The purpose of this research is to provide a diagnostic tool for local churches.

Our intent is to provide a diagnostic tool for churches that is equivalent to the finest marketplace research tool at a fraction of the marketplace cost. This is "applied" research rather than "pure" research, meaning that its intent is to provide actionable insights for church leaders, not to create social science findings for academic journals.

In a nutshell, while we intend to reinforce our research base with longitudinal studies, we chose to draw conclusions about what people need and want from the church and from their senior pastor based on point-in-time research using appropriate statistical analyses. This approach meets the most rigorous standards of market research that routinely influences decision making at some of the most respected and successful organizations in the country.

3. *Research is an* art *as well as a* science.

While the data underlying our findings is comprehensive and compelling as science, we have also benefited from the art of experts whose judgment comes from years of experience. The three research experts closest to this work represent more than fifty years of wide-ranging applied research projects. Eric Arnson began his career in quantitative consumer science at Procter & Gamble, and ultimately became the North American leader of brand strategy for McKinsey and Company. Terry Schweizer spent twenty years with the largest custom-market research organization in the world, running its Chicago office before joining the REVEAL team full-time in 2007. Nancy K. Scammacca holds a Ph.D. in quantitative methods from the University of Texas at Austin. She has served part-time on the pastoral staff of a local church for the past seven years while consulting on research projects in education and the social sciences. Eric, Terry and Nancy poured the benefit of their expertise and judgment into every finding in this book, which gives us confidence that both the art and the science components of our research are on very solid ground.

A Note about the Pie Charts

The pie charts on pages 35 and 61 that depict the relative influence of different factors on what people want from the church and the senior pastor to grow spiritually were created based on regression analyses. These analyses identified the unique influence of each independent (or predictor) variable in the analysis on the dependent (or outcome) variable, with other independent variables in the analysis held constant. While this procedure helps us see how much each predictor variable influences the outcome variable, it doesn't account for 100 percent of the factors that predict it. Other variables that we either didn't or can't measure also are involved. So the pie charts represent the sum total of the known effect of the predictor variables on the outcome variable (not including the effect of other, unmeasured variables). The magnitude of this known effect (which is called the "total variance accounted for") ranged from about 60 to 70 percent across the analyses presented in this book.

A Note about the Analysis of the Senior Pastor's Impact Through Preaching and Through Leading the Church

The results covered in chapter 4—about how the senior pastor impacts satisfaction with the church through teaching and leading—came from path analysis. This analysis was conducted to test the model depicted in chart A3-1. In this model, satisfaction with the senior's pastor effectiveness in providing spiritual challenge is mediated along two paths to determine satisfaction with the church's role in spiritual growth.

Chart A3-1

The Path Model of the Senior Pastor's Impact on Satisfaction with the Church's Role in Spiritual Growth

On the left side of the chart, satisfaction with spiritual challenge is mediated through satisfaction with preaching and vision casting. The total effect for the path from spiritual challenge through preaching and vision casting to satisfaction with the church's role in spiritual growth is 0.12.

On the right side of the chart, satisfaction with spiritual challenge is mediated through satisfaction with the spiritual guidance aspect of the church to satisfaction with the church's role in spiritual growth. The total effect for this path is 0.48 (four times the effect of the preaching path). The total variance accounted for in satisfaction with the church's role in spiritual growth by this model is 61.5 percent. In path analysis, models are evaluated using several different goodness-of-fit indices. The fit of this model was adequate to good on these indices, which, coupled with the size of our database, gives us confidence in the accuracy of these findings.

Research Standards

In summary, we have employed the highest applied research standards available, including a robust qualitative process and four waves of quantitative surveys across hundreds of diverse churches. While there is much more work yet to do, we are confident that the insights and findings in *Focus* reflect a very high level of research excellence.

WHO ARE THE 376 CHURCHES?

The findings in *Focus* are based on 376 churches surveyed in September 2008–March 2009. What follows is a brief overview of these churches.

Geography and Size

Charts A4-1 and A4-2 (page 114) show the distribution of the 376 churches by geographic location and by size (based on weekend adult attendance).

Chart A4-1

Geographic Location of the 376 Churches

Geographic Region of US	Geographic Section	Percentage of the 376 Churches Surveyed
Northeast	New England	2%
	Middle Atlantic	8%
Midwest	East North Central	29%
	West North Central	12%
South	South Atlantic	16%
	East South Central	4%
	East South Central	11%
West	Mountain	6%
	Pacific	12%

Three out of the four geographic regions account for 90 percent of the churches, with the Midwest accounting for just over 40 percent. The Midwest is more strongly represented due to the influence of the states of Illinois, Michigan and Ohio. The Northeast accounts for only 10 percent of the churches.

Weekend attendance shows a distribution concentrated in the midsize range of church size. Almost half (49 percent) report weekend attendance between 250–999 adults and 32 percent are in the smallest categories (under 250). We realize this is not necessarily representative of the national distribution of all churches, since a much higher percentage of all churches falls in the under-100 range.

Chart A4-2

Weekend Adult Attendance of the 376 Churches

Weekend Adult Attendance	Percentage of the 376 Churches Surveyed
Less than 100	4%
100 – 249	28%
250 – 499	24%
500 – 999	30%
1,000 – 2,499	11%
2,500 – 4,999	3%
5,000 or more	<1%

Denominations and Styles

Churches in the survey represent a wide mix of denominations and styles (charts A4-3 and A4-4, page 116). Nondenominational and Baptist churches account for over 40 percent of the 376 churches, though we did achieve a solid mix of other denominations, like Methodist and Presbyterian. The style descriptions reflect the three words chosen by each participating church as those that best describe their church. Contemporary, evangelical and seeker friendly lead the

Chart A4-3

Denominations Represented in the 376 Churches

Church Denominations	Percentage of the 376 Churches Surveyed
Nondenominational	29%
Baptist	13%
Methodist	9%
Presbyterian / Reformed	7%
Christian / Church of Christ	6%
Assembly of God / Church of God / Pentecostal	4%
Lutheran	4%
Brethren	2%
Christian and Missionary Alliance	2%
Nazarene	2%
Evangelical Covenant	2%
Wesleyan	2%
Other	18%

way as the most popular choices, though it is important to point out that a large percentage of churches *did not* describe themselves as contemporary, evangelical or seeker friendly.

In summary, the demographic mix of the 376 churches included in the findings reported in *Focus* represents the diversity of churches that have subscribed to the REVEAL Spiritual Life Survey since it was first made available in 2007. It was not weighted or redistributed in any way to create a particular profile.

Chart A4-4

Styles Represented in the 376 Churches

Church Style*	Percentage of the 376 Churches Surveyed
Evangelical	66%
Contemporary	61%
Sensitive to Seekers (Seeker Friendly)	49%
Missionary-minded	40%
Innovative	29%
Visionary	27%
Conservative	27%
Traditional	19%
Mainline	16%
Multicultural	11%

* Multiple responses were possible. Each church chose up to three descriptors.

WHAT IS THE REVEAL SPIRITUAL LIFE SURVEY?

The Spiritual Life Survey is a proven way to benchmark and track spiritual growth in a congregation. It moves beyond measures like attendance and financial giving to determine if your church is really making a difference helping people become more like Christ. This anonymous, congregational online survey is easy to understand, simple to administer and repeatable over time to monitor change. Its large database of 235,000 congregants from over 850 churches lets you compare your results with other churches.

Should My Church Use This Tool?

When it comes to spiritual growth, we need to be able to measure the unseen. Churches who use the Spiritual Life Survey receive an in-depth understanding of their congregants' spiritual attitudes, motivations, behaviors and satisfaction. The survey enables church leaders to track over time the movement of their congregation toward Christ, to see if ministry efforts and resource allocations are really contributing to the spiritual health of people in the church.

What Does the Spiritual Life Survey Provide?

- **Three surveys over five years:** a baseline survey and two follow-up surveys. Follow-up surveys can be executed at any time within the five-year window.
- **A Spiritual Life diagnostic report,** benchmarking your church's spiritual profile against the results of any prior surveys as well as other churches in the REVEAL database.
- **Marketing collateral** to help promote the Spiritual Life Survey to your congregation, including sample text for print and e-mail communication and other tools to increase awareness and participation.

What Pastors Are Saying about the
(REVEAL) Spiritual Life Survey

I do believe, as Bill Hybels says, that "Feedback is the breakfast of champions." The REVEAL Spiritual Life Survey helped us stop guessing where our people are in their walk with Christ and is helping us rethink and restrategize how to best help them move forward.

Kent Williams | senior pastor
Christian Fellowship Church
Ashburn, Virginia

Whether the REVEAL results are what you had hoped to see or not, you will gain insight into your church's spiritual life and be able to respond to reality rather than to your own impressions or wishful thinking.

Mark Schultz | lead pastor
Peace Lutheran Church
Eau Claire, Wisconsin

As the old saying goes, "Facts are our friends." Getting the facts—and not just sanctified opinions or guesses—about the nature of our congregation's life with God was well worth the time, the money and the raised eyebrows.

Glenn McDonald | senior pastor
Zionsville Presbyterian Church
Zionsville, Indiana

The REVEAL Spiritual Life Survey can help you more effectively make disciples by providing honest, objective feedback from your congregation. As a senior pastor, you may know that something isn't working, but not know exactly what "it" is. REVEAL can help.

David Johnson | lead pastor
Kalamazoo Community Church
Kalamazoo, Michigan

Although it's one of the most vulnerable and authentic action steps you will do as the spiritual leader of your church, this will test your sincere desire to be the best leader you can be for your church.

Brian Yost | lead pastor
South Shore Community Church
Sarasota, Florida

The REVEAL Spiritual Life Survey was a real eye-opener in helping me evaluate where our church actually is. It provided the foundation for strategic considerations in the development of the ministry.

John Crandall | senior pastor
Life Pointe Church, Woodland, California

REVEAL is an amazing way of measuring the true spiritual temperature of your congregation. You may not like the results, but you will be thankful for the candid accuracy of its findings.

Dr. Deron K. Boyer | senior pastor
Northwest United Methodist Church
Peoria, Illinois

Confirm your hunches or be blown away with the objective data the REVEAL Spiritual Life Survey provides.

Joshua Kim | pastor
Stanwich Congregational Church
Greenwich, Connecticut

REVEAL has helped us tremendously in identifying ways to make the greatest impact in the lives of those who trust us with their spiritual guidance. We now have trustworthy evidence of strengths and weaknesses, as well as goals to pursue.

Daniel Harris | director of discipleship
First Methodist Church of Midland
Midland, Texas

This material, the books and the survey data, have been the most enlightening and energizing material we have used. The focus is not on church growth but church health, and the survey report gives very practical insights that provide guidance for helping people to become more like Christ. God has used REVEAL to raise spiritual passion for God to the highest level I've seen in my twenty-nine years as pastor of this church.

Bob Wine | senior pastor
New Life Assembly, Kearney, Nebraska

ABOUT
THE AUTHORS

Greg L. Hawkins

Greg L. Hawkins is executive pastor of Willow Creek Community Church. Since 1996, he has assisted Senior Pastor Bill Hybels in providing strategic leadership to Willow Creek's five campuses and to the Willow Creek Association. He also serves as point leader for REVEAL, an initiative within the WCA that utilizes research tools and discoveries to help churches better understand spiritual growth in their congregations. Prior to joining the staff of Willow Creek in 1991, Greg spent five years as a consultant for McKinsey & Company. He has an undergraduate degree in civil engineering from Texas A&M University and an MBA from Stanford University. Greg and his wife, Lynn, live in the Chicago suburbs with their three children.

Cally Parkinson

Cally Parkinson is brand manager for REVEAL, an initiative within the WCA that utilizes research tools and discoveries to help churches better understand spiritual growth in their congregations. She previously served as the director of communication services at Willow Creek Community Church, a role she took on following a twenty-five-year career at Allstate Insurance Company. At Allstate, Cally held a number of different director- and officer-level positions in strategic planning, research, finance and communications. She has a BA in languages from Depauw University and a master's degree from the American Graduate School of International Management. Cally and her husband, Rich, live in the Chicago suburbs and have two grown children.

revealnow.com

We want to hear from you. The purpose of REVEAL research is to provide church leaders with fact-based, actionable insights about spiritual growth. Your feedback is vital to our ongoing work. We encourage you to send us your questions and comments—about this resource or about anything else related to REVEAL. Direct your communications to cally@revealnow.com. Thank you!

VISION, TRAINING, AND RESOURCES FOR PREVAILING CHURCHES

This resource was created to serve you and to help you build a local church that prevails. It is just one of many ministry tools published by the Willow Creek Association.

The Willow Creek Association (WCA) was created in 1992 to serve a rapidly growing number of churches from across the denominational spectrum that are committed to helping unchurched people become fully devoted followers of Christ. Membership in the WCA now numbers over 12,000 Member Churches worldwide from more than ninety denominations.

The Willow Creek Association links like-minded Christian leaders with each other and with strategic vision, training and resources in order to help them build prevailing churches designed to reach their redemptive potential.

For specific information about WCA conferences, resources, membership and other ministry services contact:

WILLOW

Willow Creek Association
P.O. Box 3188 • Barrington, IL 60011-3188 • Phone: 847-570-9812 • Fax: 847-765-5046
www.willowcreek.com